Understanding Persons

Personal and Impersonal Relationships

F.M. BERENSON

Head of Philosophy,
Stockwell College, London

THE HARVESTER PRESS

First published in Great Britain in 1981 by
THE HARVESTER PRESS LIMITED
Publisher: John Spiers
16 Ship Street, Brighton, Sussex

© F.M. Berenson, 1981

British Library Cataloguing in Publication Data

Berenson, F M
    Understanding persons.
    1. Interpersonal relations
    I. Title
    128'.4   HM132

    ISBN 0-85527-463-8

Printed in Great Britain by Bristol Typesetting Co. Ltd,
Barton Manor, St. Philips, Bristol

This b
Books m:
(

Understanding Persons

Personal and Impersonal Relationships

HARVESTER STUDIES IN PHILOSOPHY

General Editor: Margaret A. Boden,
Reader in Philosophy and Psychology, University of Sussex

To Joe, Richard and Nobbie

Contents

Preface

THIS book is, in a modest way, an essay in the vast subject of the Philosophy of Personal Relationships. My main aim is to bring out the conceptual significance of the notion of human relationships and how these link up with the possibility of understanding persons and with understanding the self.

Since Wittgenstein, one of the major concerns of philosophy has been with the notion of objectivity and the vital role it plays in making knowledge possible. More recently the formal approach to the concept of meaning has been the fashion, an approach which makes no reference to understanding. The topic of personal understanding and personal relationships has therefore receded into the background. This book offers what may, with reservations, be described as an attempt to redress the balance in some very small measure.

The idea of a Philosophy of Personal Relationships is liable to be met with a degree of scepticism by some philosophers as it is not immediately obvious how and whether this subject lends itself to philosophical treatment. I try to approach the issue by posing the philosophical question: 'How is it possible that human beings come to understand each other in various degrees in spite of the problems inherent in what human beings are?' My approach to this question is via an analysis of issues arising from our attempts at understanding other persons and ourselves. My aim is to look at the issue in a way which is not based on the familiar private/public or internal/external distinctions.

In attempting to treat analytically the concept of human relationships and of understanding within them it is not necessarily the correct move to search for a strict statement of the necessary and sufficient conditions of its application; modern analytic philosophy has tended to give a purely intellectual account of personal relationships. By the very nature of such relationships, which are rich in all kinds of emotional attitudes, to try to give a strictly academic account is to blind oneself to important facts about our form of life.

Persons, after all, are 'entities' who stand in relationships and to be something as a person must involve understanding something of these relationships. This is not just an academic matter and could not characteristically be so. Hence we should not construe the understanding of a person in a certain way as one thing and separate from the feelings that we have. Many of the central features of human agency cannot be understood independently of a connection with the emotions. For a philosopher the problem is one of how to describe this kind of understanding in general terms. This is the task I have set myself.

The first chapter is introductory. I discuss what is involved in understanding a situation, showing how different kinds of understanding are possible. An argument is set out to show why Popper's specific account of situation understanding is inadequate for any real understanding of persons. However, his general thesis that all understanding is situation understanding and that propositions are primary candidates for understanding seems to me to be a useful and attractive one. I outline an alternative account and conclude that there is necessarily something propositional about understanding which makes situations the paradigmatic subject matter of understanding in that what a situation involves can and must be seen in propositional terms.

I then focus on persons in situations and discuss difficulties arising from psychological explanations in the area of understanding individual people and underline certain profound disagreements between psychologists of different schools, also sketching suggested new directions for psychological explanation.

One of the main characteristics of understanding persons is that much of such understanding is not transferable to another person in a way in which we can transfer previous knowledge and understanding of things. Each person demands a very particular and often unique kind of understanding. A preliminary discussion of what is involved in this kind of understanding is offered.

In Chapter 2 I argue that situations qualify particularly as objects of understanding and I extend this notion to specific fields in order to see whether all understanding can be taken as situation understanding. The question I pose is: To what extent is our understanding immediately objective and to what extent do we extract from our own experience a great deal which illuminates our understanding? An argument is offered to show that in any case of understanding, two kinds of understanding are involved, the objective and the personal. I then go on to concentrate on the personal aspects of understanding and I do this in a Merleau-Pontian context in that I try to apply (with modifications) his account of perception of objects in general, and music in particular, to the understanding of persons.

A situation which one is trying to understand implies a given person's involvement in it, not merely to the extent that the situation imposes itself on the person concerned but, as importantly, what the given person contributes to it in his attempts to understand. In trying to understand a situation we extract and contribute to a greater or lesser extent and the mode of involvement is based to a large extent on subjective elements within the objective framework. I discuss, via an example taken from Proust, those aspects which we .extract from our experience which illuminate our understanding. These represent our personal contribution to understanding. Thus, in arguing that situations qualify particularly as objects of understanding, I stress the importance of subjective elements which every person brings to such understanding; how a person contributes and what he extracts. The degree and kind of involvement regulates the degree and kind of understanding. It is for this reason that I speak of perception and understanding as a creative process within the context of reciprocity which is set up between perceiver and perceived; in the context which is tantamount to a situation having been set up.

Given the above argument, the understanding of persons has to be investigated in terms of kinds of situations which are set up in various cases. The notion of reciprocity which brings out personal elements is crucial in the particular context of person understanding and must form a significant part of any such investigation. The notion of reciprocity takes on great importance in reference to persons and is, therefore, discussed extensively in following chapters.

Chapter 3 is an exposition of a positive theory of understanding persons in the course of which important distinctions are drawn and an analysis of the concept of the personal is offered. The notion of relationships is looked at in detail. I begin by analysing the crucial distinction between personal/impersonal and that between subject/object. It is very tempting to suppose that since our contact with other persons is different from any contact with objects, therefore every such encounter is in this sense personal. This way of looking at the issue is inadequate because it leaves no room for the contrast between personal/ impersonal or rather creates a seeming paradox that a relation between two persons may be both personal and impersonal at the same time. I go on to discuss in detail what is involved here in terms of first and second level concepts where the first level amounts to having the concept 'person' and the second level involves in addition having the concept of what it is for someone to be a person of a particular kind. I then go on to argue that any real understanding of a person is only possible when one stands in relation to him both as object and as subject. We can rule out here seeing a person purely as an object, i.e., material object, because to do so would be to fail to have an adequate conception of what a person is, of failing to apply any first level concepts.

The question which arises is whether any kind of personal acquaintance qualifies as a personal relationship of some kind and, further, what is involved in the notion of personal relationships. I attempt to answer by first discussing Strawson's distinction between an objective and subjective attitude and enlarge on his argument that a purely objective attitude to another person is impossible to sustain under normal circumstances and why this is so.

I then go on to explain the difference between impersonal and personal relationships which leads me to distinguish between degrees of personal understanding and to point out what understanding another on a deep level involves. Thus I argue that knowing a certain number of characteristics of a given person and a number of facts about him does not constitute a real understanding of the person concerned. This kind of knowledge can be obtained in a variety of ways but the person, about whom information of this kind is come by, need only be seen as an object. Deep understanding stems from seeing a person both as object and as subject. Seeing him in this way involves having personal experience of what I refer to as his personal side and this, in turn, involves the necessity of standing in some kind of personal relationship with that person.

I try to show why I take the standing in some kind of personal relationship with a person as a necessary condition for understanding him on a deep level (personal understanding). I argue that there is a distinction between what I term personal and scientific knowledge; this distinction is one which cannot be equated with knowledge based on subjective and overt factors respectively. Personal knowledge and understanding is and has to be based on both factors. Similarly scientific knowledge based on observation and gathering of information may result in an understanding of both subjective and overt factors. But *the quality* of the understanding *is different*. It is only in reciprocal personal relationships that subjective aspects of a person's life have a chance of spontaneously and fully manifesting themselves. Attitudes, purposes and reciprocal responses are of crucial importance here. But these are lacking in cases of scientific knowledge. Thus the point here is *not* that we cannot come to know a person's subjective side in cases of scientific knowledge but rather that the resulting understanding is limited and qualitatively different. We have no experience of the reciprocal development of understanding.

Chapter 4 is a preliminary to the consideration of the view that understanding of persons is not and cannot be solely intellectual understanding but is also importantly related to emotions and feelings which arise within given relationships. In Chapter 5 an attempt is made to show that emotions play an important part in provoking our understanding and the argument is extended to show that emotions are neither necessarily passive nor irrational. In this section I try to bring out the central role which emotions and emotion concepts play both in self and other understanding thus attempting to argue why I take it as mistaken to treat of emotions as purely or necessarily passive phenomena which are also, therefore, irrational. The picture of a man which emerges from such a view seems fraught with serious conceptual difficulties. On this view we are asked to regard emotions as something that happens to a creature who would be intelligible to us as a human agent quite independently of this important emotional dimension. This, however, is to presuppose that emotions are somehow not a part of what we take a person 'really' to be. I suggest, on the contrary, that such a view is based on a misunderstanding of the concept 'person'.

Having attempted to spell out what sort of circumstances are necessary to the development of personal understanding and what is involved in the power to provoke such understanding, I offer an answer (in Chapter 6) to the question what personal understanding within personal relationships consists in and what it is that a person outside such a relationship is precluded from understanding. The answer is supplied with the aid of examples from literature.

Chapter 7 consists of some concluding remarks.

In writing this book, I have incurred more debts than I can possibly acknowledge: to my former teachers, to my students and to friends and colleagues whose ideas I have picked up and whose encouragement I have cherished. To them, my sincere thanks.

A version of this book was presented as a doctoral thesis to the University of London in 1975. I wish to express my gratitude to Professor D.W. Hamlyn for his generous supervision. He has helped me to reconsider many of my ideas, to avoid inconsistencies and to gain a better understanding of the issues raised. To my examiners, Professor J. Benson and Dr. J. Watling, very special thanks for their painstaking and most stimulating discussion of my work. They generously contributed ideas for the book version.

I am most grateful to R.K. Elliott for stimulating my interest in Merleau-Ponty, to Dr. T. Diffey for his help, encouragement and for invaluable, enthusiastic comments; to Dr. S.C. Brown, who also read the typescript and made helpful suggestions, to Mrs. M. Baldwin for her generous offer of literary examples and to my family for their wholehearted help and cooperation.

I wish, particularly, to acknowledge my debt to Dr. M.A. Boden, the editor of this series, for her sensitive understanding, guidance and always constructive, significant advice on improvements. The responsibility for the faults which remain is entirely mine.

My thanks to Miss J. Farrer for her great help in typing the manuscript.

1 Situation Understanding

WHEN Lear, in despair, rages: 'Then let them anatomise Regan; see what breeds about her heart',[1] he is echoing for all of us the difficulties inherent in understanding another person. Yet, in spite of the difficulties, human beings come to understand each other to a greater or lesser extent. The degree and kind of understanding achieved is greatly influenced by the sort of persons we are. This needs expanding and perhaps it can best be shown by first examining what is involved in understanding a given situation. I shall use for this purpose a modified version of Jean Valjean's predicament in *Les Misérables* by Victor Hugo. What took place can be stated simply—he stole a loaf of bread. Now what is involved in our understanding just this? Well, apart from having the concepts 'loaf' and 'bread' which in itself presupposes a whole string of understanding involving food, shape and so on, we also have to understand what stealing is and that, if anything, is even more complicated. As regards the former, we have to *know* what a loaf of bread is. My claiming to know what a loaf of bread is amounts to my being able to subsume what I see under the relevant concept, i.e., being able to identify it as a such and such, and this brings in understanding. Knowing what x is, is having the concept of x; understanding is presupposed here.

The next step in what is involved in understanding the situation described by the proposition 'He stole a loaf of bread' is vastly more complicated. In order to have the concept of stealing, a whole string of very complicated understanding is necessary, such as what is involved in making a moral judgment, the notion of punishment, legal institutions and so on.

One could not explain stealing to someone by simply saying that the man concerned took the loaf without paying for it. The complexities involved can perhaps best be illustrated by giving a dictionary definition of stealing: 'To take by theft, to take, gain or win by contrivance, unexpectedly, insidiously, gradually, or furtively: to snatch. . . .' (*Chambers 20th Century Dictionary*). This is not a definition in a helpful sense because the concepts of

stealing and theft are not only interdependent but internally related and therefore understanding the one is impossible without
also understanding the other. On the other hand, it is not necessary to understand *all* the expressions in the definition in order to
have a concept of stealing.

One can bring out in this connection the relevance of one's
interests to *how* one understands a situation. Supposing Valjean
is brought to trial for his offence, the task of making the jury
understand the situation is shared between the prosecutor and
counsel for the defence. Each will concentrate, however, on
explaining only those aspects of the situation which are helpful to
their respective objectives: the condemning or acquitting of the
accused. Thus other, not immediately obvious, aspects of the
situation will be brought out: why he stole the bread, what sort
of a man he is, the circumstances prevailing at the time, moral
questions as to whether the commission of an illegal act can ever
be justified and so on. Now, supposing for my purposes that
several specialists become interested in Valjean's case, and each
of them carries out a special investigation. For example, how
would a sociologist approach his case? He would probably in-
vestigate the social, political and economic conditions which gave
rise to a situation in which an otherwise honest man was forced
to steal. Beyond this, Valjean himself would probably figure as an
abstract unit, a type, a starting point of his investigations. The
sociologist's understanding of the situation would not necessarily
include trying to understand the man Valjean, only Valjean as
perhaps a historical figure. His understanding would be largely
confined to discovering 'that so and so is the case'. Added to this
understanding 'that', would be an investigation, a search for an
answer to the question 'how' such and such could have occurred.
In this particular case the 'understanding how' would be very
closely related to, be a part of, the understanding 'that' involved.
The understanding 'how' is not the kind involved in the understanding of how to perform a skill, but an understanding how x
came about, in a sense more akin to understanding 'why', which
might yield causal explanations.

Thus another aspect of what is involved in understanding a
situation is that which goes with theoretical explanations which
attempt to give an explanation of the causes as well as the consequences. A situation can be seen not only as what the situation

actually is but in terms of what gave rise to it and what its consequences may be. Now, if I take my original example as part of a wider situation—the French revolution—several explanations of it may be offered. Someone may offer an explanation in terms of the Marxist theory which would comprehensively cover all three above-mentioned aspects of the French revolution. But someone else may, perhaps, offer a Freudian explanation which, in a different way, would also partially cover the relevant aspects. The contents of understanding may be different yet each is an understanding of the situation.

I have concentrated so far on how a sociologist might view the described situation in order to bring out certain kinds of possible understanding which may differ from other kinds; it is not the factual (objective) description of the situation which is at stake but the fact that particular interests may influence which aspects of a given situation we try to understand. By contrast with those mentioned above, an artist's understanding may be very different again because he will probably look for different considerations. He may be struck by the expression on Valjean's face and try to interpret it on canvas. He will probably be concerned with the man Valjean, the individual—his feelings, thoughts, motives and his suffering. Someone looking at the situation in retrospect might be able to understand certain features of it which could not be apparent at the time, for instance, the way in which it fits into a wider historical context. He might thus see additional implications.

A situation consists of a more or less complex set of circumstances, each of which may require different kinds of understanding, some of which a given person may be quite incapable of having. It is also necessary to take into account the fact that degrees of understanding are possible. Thus I may already be said to understand a situation to some extent if I can describe what took place in the sense of giving the facts, of enumerating a sequence of events. This represents understanding a situation on a most superficial level. On a more complex level, motives, desires, ways of coping, intentions, moral or religious attitudes, beliefs, reactions and all sorts of considerations of this kind may be involved in our understanding of a given situation. To complicate the issue further, the reasoning of the person involved in the situation has to be taken into account—how he views what is taking place, which may or may not be my understanding of the elements of the situation. The web of understanding becomes extremely complex. Yet I may be said to understand the situation whether it is on a superficial level or whether my understanding encompasses many of the complexities involved. The difference lies in the degree or depth of understanding involved.

That is not to say that the only possible differences are differences in degree, because understanding an additional aspect of a situation may change our understanding in that it involves putting a different interpretation on it or results in our understanding it differently from someone else. It is not sufficient to hold that having been able to describe the situation correctly and having understood the person or persons involved I now have what may be termed a complete understanding of the situation. This would involve not only an approach from all possible points of view but also understanding complete histories and consequences of all the different elements. For ordinary purposes we have to fall back on considerations of what my interests are in the situation and which factors are in that case necessary for my understanding of it. Each kind of understanding contributes to the general understanding of the situation which is many-sided. It is already clear, at this stage, that there are many different *kinds* of understanding possible. This is due not merely to the many-sidedness of a situation itself but also because different approaches are possible. Spinoza said that the particular way in which we form our concepts is not only accidental (through sense perception) but is also affected by our interests, desires and purposes.

It is the task of, e.g., scientists to provide us with a better understanding of our world and thus of various situations which occur within it. But there are many other disciplines whose task is equally to provide better understanding. Historians, theologians, artists, philosophers, etc., all share in the scientist's task but it is important to stress the crucial difference between them—that although they all try to provide a better understanding of our world, their objectives, their points of view and the ways in which they seek better understanding, are different. Thus each would view Valjean's situation differently. Some would direct their explanations at the situation as an 'objective' object, as, for example, the sociologist's approach. Others would concentrate on Valjean himself as a unique person and therefore in a unique situation. The important distinction between them is that the former would only attempt to understand Valjean as an agent, a type, in order to ensure 'objectivity' and such an approach calls into question the very possibility of understanding Valjean, the person.

A qualification is needed here. I may have given the impression that any explanation is as good or as valid as any other. Obviously not just any explanation will do. If two explanations are incompatible then we know that at least one of them is wrong. I shall discuss various criteria of what is to count as an understanding of a person or a situation throughout this book but at this stage some very general remarks about explanation are called for.

Difficulties arise out of theory-bound explanations in this context in that, e.g., a Marxist or a Freudian in offering an explanation of Valjean's situation is attempting to fit the situation into a ready and very specific conceptual matrix and then to draw certain analogies and implications. The understanding achieved in this way is only as successful as the matrix used. We are usually in a position to judge whether an explanation which is offered is acceptable or not. But there are cases where such judgments are not possible as in Freudian explanation which it is impossible to evaluate because there is no way in which it could be checked. In such cases it is a matter of individual choice or preference or success in treatment whether we accept it as a possible explanation or not.

The evaluation of theory-bound explanations is important in our context particularly for personality theorists and clinical psychologists whose task it is to find matrices which will enable them to achieve a better understanding of people. I shall return to this point in detail.

Ultimately we need to decide whether each case is a case of understanding, possible understanding, misunderstanding or a complete failure to understand; allowing for exceptional cases where no such decision is possible. Such exceptions are not exclusive to understanding as opposed to knowledge. In the words of the well-known hymn: 'I know that my Redeemer liveth', we raise the same problem as regards knowledge.

I have given this rather sketchy preliminary example of what may be involved in understanding a situation in order to bring out what I mean by saying that our understanding of a situation depends to a great extent on the sort of person we are and consequently on our desires, purposes and interests.

Before attempting to give a full account of situation understanding it will be useful to look at some prevalent kinds of explanation which seem, on the face of it, to be particularly relevant; one is Popper's theory of hermeneutics.

1.1(a) Hermeneutics

Hermeneutics is a theory of the principles of understanding and interpretation particularly in historical explanation. Some philosophers, e.g., Dilthey, extended this notion to encompass understanding of individuals conceived as 'the greatest reality' in history and, therefore, the greatest reality we can know. Popper's definition extends to a theory of all possible kinds of understanding which he equates with 'Geisteswissenschaften'. It is as a result of this claim that we need to look at Popper's account in some detail.

For Popper, hermeneutics in all fields, including the humanities, has as its basis the understanding of problem situations. Understanding of persons is also tantamount to the understanding of a problem situation; this is because, for Popper, there is no qualitative difference between understanding men and understanding nature. Popper expresses the issue involved in understanding a problem situation as follows:

. . ., without taking the words 'world' or 'universe' too seriously, we may distinguish the following three worlds or universes: first, the world of physical objects or of physical states; secondly, the world of states of consciousness, or of mental states, or perhaps of behavioural dispositions to act; and thirdly, the world of *objective contents of thought*, especially of scientific and poetic thoughts and of works of art.[2]

He goes on to say that it is impossible to understand the human mind and the human self without understanding the third world and employing its methods.

Now, employing third-world methods involves operations with objects belonging to the objective third world. These objects are problems, theories, conjectures, critical arguments, etc., objects which exist independently of the knowing subject or the subject who created them—they have become objectified, i.e., acquired publicity and no longer exist merely in the second world of the subject's (their respective creators') mind. Third-world objects have become autonomous in this sense; these are objects which are 'on record' as it were. Problem situations, which belong to the third world, can only be understood by an application of objective methods. The activity of understanding consists, essentially, in operating with third-world objects and using objective methods based on the deductive model. The operation consists of imaginative conjectures and refutations in the course of problem-solving; in this context the problem is whatever is to be understood. The schematic form which Popper offers us is this:

$$P_1 \rightarrow TT \rightarrow EE \rightarrow P_2$$

where P_1 stands for the initial problem, TT stands for 'tentative theory', i.e., the imaginative conjectural solution which amounts to a first attempt at a tentative interpretation. EE stands for 'error elimination', i.e., a severe critical examination of the tentative interpretation. This step involves the critical use of documentary evidence, competing theories or conjectures or, in other words, the critical employment of third-world objects. P_2 is the problem situation as it emerges from the first critical attempt to solve P_1. This process is repeated until the interpretation or conjectural theory reached finds support in the fact that it can throw new light on new problems or, alternatively, if it finds support in the fact that it explains many sub-problems; it is at some such stage that a satisfactory understanding is reached.

The above formula is identical with the one employed in Popper's scientific methodology. Popper wishes to abolish any distinction between scientific and psychological explanations of understanding, i.e., between methods employed in science and hermeneutics respectively, by arguing that we cannot reach any kind of valid explanation in any sphere of enquiry without employing scientific methodology.

The final 'state' of understanding both in science and the humanities is the interpretation of the problem situation. Thus Popper writes:

So every interpretation is a kind of *theory* and, like every theory, it is anchored in other theories, and in other third-world objects. And in this way the third-world problem of the *merits* of the interpretation can be raised and discussed, . . . But even the subjective act . . . of 'understanding' can be understood, in its turn, only through its connections with third-world objects. For I assert the following three theses concerning the subjective act of understanding.

(1) That every subjective act of understanding is largely anchored in the third world;

(2) that almost all important remarks which can be made about such an act consist in pointing out its relations to third-world objects; and

(3) that such an act consists in the main of operations with third-world objects: . . . almost as if they were physical objects.

This, I suggest, can be generalised, and holds for every subjective act of 'knowledge': all the important things we can say about an act of knowledge consist of pointing out the third-world objects of the act—a theory or proposition—and its relation to other third-world objects, such as the arguments bearing on the problem as well as the objects known.[3]

Popper mentions the subject of emotions in passing and it is rather significant that 'emotions' do not appear in the index of the book. His analysis amounts to saying that he is ready to admit that there are certain subjective experiences or attitudes which do play a part in the process of understanding—these are matters of emphasis only, e.g., the picking out of a problem or a theory as important or, conversely, the dismissal of some theory as irrelevant. Such proposals are conveyed by expressive and emotional means. Nevertheless, he states quite unequivocally that his central thesis is that any *significant* analysis of understanding has to proceed by analysing third-world objects. All else, such as descriptions of our subjective feelings, '. . . may be very interesting, but has little bearing on our problem; . . .' He stresses that his sketchy analysis of some emotional overtones attempts to illustrate the claim that even such overtones may sometimes be best understood in terms of third-world objects.

This claim should not be confounded with an even more important one—that the task of explaining psychological states such as emotions creates its own theoretical problems, to be solved by its own tentative theories: theories (that is, third-world objects) about the second world. Yet this should not be taken to mean that we can understand persons solely, or mainly, by studying psychological theories about them; . . . in all understanding, including the understanding of persons and their actions, . . . the analysis of third-world situations is our paramount task.[4]

He also asserts that we can learn more about the psychology of research by studying theories than by any direct behaviouristic, dispositional or psychological approach. In general, we may learn a great deal more about behaviour and psychology from the study of the products. Popper goes on to say:

In what follows I will call the approach from the side of the products —the theories and the arguments—the 'objective' approach or the 'third-world' approach. And I will call the behaviourist, the psychological, . . . approach to scientific knowledge the 'subjective' approach or the 'second-world' approach.[5]

Thus Popper's main point is that actions can be explained as problem-solving via his analysis of the schema of conjectures and refutations ($P_1 \rightarrow TT \rightarrow EE \rightarrow P_2$).

It becomes clear that psychological theories are inferior to other theories because they are theories about 'mental states' and thus about second-world objects. For this reason they cannot be as objectively based as theories about actions can, i.e., theories about overt behaviour (the product) which can be objectively assessed. But then much of psychological theory *is* about actions, so we seem to end up with an unresolvable tension inherent in Popper's account. He does say, however, that the difference between his approach and psychological approaches is that he advocates theories about products (effects) while psychology is more concerned with causes. His situational analysis in this context consists of a tentative or conjectural explanation of some human action in terms of, what he calls, the rationality principle. Each rational action can be explained rationally by the application of the principle. Problems and their solutions are objective—the rationality principle says that the agent confronted with a problem situation will act in a way that is 'appropriate' to the solving of the problem. All human action can be seen in those terms.

Popper sums up his thesis, in the above context, as follows:

By a situational analysis I mean a certain kind of tentative or conjectural explanation of some human action which appeals to the situation in which the agent finds himself. . . . In other words, our schema of problem-solving by conjecture and refutation or a similar schema may be used as an explanatory theory of human actions, since we can interpret an action as an attempt to solve a problem. Thus the explanatory theory of action will, in the main, consist of a conjectural reconstruction of the problem and its background. *A theory of this kind may well be testable.*[6] (My italics.)

Now this last point is very strange indeed. Since refutation is a necessary condition of the process (as stated in his schema) of problem-solving and thus understanding, we cannot award any interpretation the status of theory *unless* that theory is testable by the application of his general criterion of falsifiability. Thus any objective theory is a theory about third-world objects if, and only if, it is falsifiable and, therefore, also testable.

The implication is that any areas of enquiry which do not lend themselves to the above methodology cannot be seriously considered as candidates for knowledge nor for understanding of any objective kind whatsoever. I shall argue that this is too narrow a view of understanding as applied to persons in situations. Our attempts to understand another person cannot be legitimately limited to the employment of such a methodology on the grounds that it is *the only* method which will secure objectivity.

How can we apply Popper's formula to understanding Valjean's situation? What makes his situation unique is not just the factual aspect of it, i.e., the action which can be described by the statement: He stole a loaf of bread. The uniqueness of the situation is inextricably bound up with the fact that it is Valjean's situation rather than someone else's and our understanding of what that implies, what difference that makes to the situation, is crucial. It seems clear from Popper's account that any theory we formulate must be a theory about Valjean's action, not about Valjean's state of mind, feelings, emotions, etc. Any theory one may put forward or any solution to the problem has to be formulated in language and then tested and discussed. It can be argued about, attacked, defended, used without reference to the person who put it forward; here Popper underlines the importance of the role of language in objectifying our ideas.

But the difficulty about how we apply this to Valjean's predica-

ment remains. Supposing, as is the case, Valjean does not put
forward any 'theories' in his defence. How then can we objectify
what the situation means to him, the person that he is? The short
answer, in Popper's view, is that this is not our concern; our
concern is with third-world objects only—in this case Valjean's
action itself. Beyond this, it is difficult to see how persons in
situations can be objects belonging to the objective third world in
Popper's sense. The crucial criterion of the status of third-world
objects is that they exist independently of the knowing subject or
the subject who created them. The situation in which Valjean
finds himself is certainly one which has acquired publicity and no
longer exists exclusively in his mind (whatever that means), but it
makes no sense to say that the situation is, therefore, independent
of the thinking and feeling subject Valjean whose thoughts and
emotions are inextricably bound up with it. Indeed, I shall argue
that they are an inseparable, integral part of the situation, as
Valjean's situation. I therefore fail to see how one could justify
Popper's claim that he is concerned with the understanding of
individual persons as opposed to understanding what people *do*,
in general, when confronted with any given situation.

These arguments notwithstanding, Popper's notion that all
understanding is situation understanding is, I think, a useful and
attractive one, and could well repay pursuing it further. Let us,
therefore, examine his statement that theories or propositions, or
statements are the most important linguistic third-world objective
entities. These entities are objects of understanding. In the light
of this statement, let us begin by attempting to spell out what is
involved in understanding a proposition.

1.1(b) Understanding a Proposition

To begin with, I wish to make a general point about knowledge
and understanding. Aristotle assimilates understanding to right
thinking.[7] He also implies that knowledge is included in the
process of right thinking and is, thus, a part of thinking. He is not,
however, engaged in sorting out these concepts separately, thereby,
I think, implicitly drawing attention to their close relationship.

Because of the obviously close relationship between knowledge
and understanding it would, I think, be misguided to look for any
clear-cut, definitive distinctions between them; certainly not any

distinctions that would apply generally for all cases of knowledge and understanding. In saying that it would be misguided to look for definitive distinctions I am not, here, making an assumption; the statement is based on my attempts to find possible distinctions and my failure to find any of significance. As a result, I shall concentrate on understanding as such and deal with any possible distinctions as, and when, these arise.

A proposition could not make sense unless it was either true or false, but understanding a proposition is not a question of knowing how to verify it, only of understanding its sense. It involves understanding the concepts which enter into the proposition and being able to distinguish what is said from nonsense which has no truth value. We can be said to understand a proposition without knowing whether it is true or false, but if it is intelligible, if it has sense, then it has to be either true or false.

Knowing its truth value places that which the proposition expresses in the realm of knowledge—in such cases I know that the proposition is true (I, therefore, possess some particular knowledge of something). But to possess propositional knowledge presupposes understanding the proposition in question. That there is a very close relationship here seems obvious but, at the same time, we cannot substitute 'I know proposition p' for 'I understand proposition p' without changing something from sense to nonsense. This is an example of a case (where the object is a proposition) where, though one can understand something, speaking of knowledge does not make sense. (There are certain exceptions to my general point—cases where it would make sense to speak in terms of knowing a proposition, e.g., 'Do you know Smith's proposition that . . .'—but this is a very special usage.) There is a certain oddity in speaking of knowing and understanding a proposition; the correct account, I think, is that one understands a proposition and knows its truth value. Understanding a proposition involves understanding what would be the case if it were true and having the concepts expressed in the proposition. We are concerned here with what it is one understands.

Further, knowing and understanding a fact involves knowing and understanding that which the proposition expresses. But understanding the fact which the proposition expresses is an understanding of what is being said and that understanding is presupposed in any possibility of knowing the fact which the proposition expresses. Thus knowing a fact presupposes understanding, whereas understanding the proposition which states the fact does not presuppose knowing the fact as a fact. Understanding a proposition is equivalent to understanding its sense, understanding what is said.

An important qualification is needed here. In cases where one fails to understand a proposition it would be wrong to conclude from this alone that it lacks sense. In some cases I may need some explanation of what another means by his statement. His explanation may or may not be enough for my understanding of it. I am also limited in my understanding in other ways. For example, I may not understand certain foreign languages because they are not within the scope of my knowledge. We have, in this context, to take cognisance of the fact of personal limits of knowledge and understanding (in this case, of propositions). What I know and understand is what I can normally express and understand by means of language. I am here speaking of *my* understanding of a given proposition and since *my* understanding is limited, my failure to understand a proposition is no guarantee that the proposition lacks sense, only that it lacks sense for me. Given an adequate explanation I may come to understand it; the point is that it must be in a form which can be understood by someone, not necessarily by me. What, I think, emerges at this point is that understanding is normally presupposed in any case of propositional knowledge.

Having said this, we must recognise that the understanding, which is presupposed in cases of propositional knowledge, may itself involve knowledge, although not knowledge that the given proposition is true or knowledge of the fact which the proposition expresses. This could be put differently by saying that in order to know x, I must understand y; but y may equally be an object of knowledge although different from knowledge of x. In order to know the fact which the proposition 'The cat is on the mat' expresses, I must understand what is being said, understand its sense. But in order to understand its sense I must understand the concepts which enter into the proposition and this, in itself, involves knowing what cats and mats are (objects of knowledge), as well as having to judge what particular knowledge to apply to the understanding of this particular proposition. This point stresses the close relationship between knowledge and understanding. The understanding presupposed in cases of propositional knowledge involves applying prior knowledge on which the understanding is based.

Now, it seems to me that since not all knowledge is propositional, this fact carries with it certain implications: understanding is, I think, essentially propositional in that the propositional nature of understanding follows from the fact that what can be understood is *normally* expressible in words. Furthermore, one cannot understand something without understanding something about it. It is not so clear that this is true of all knowledge other than propositional knowledge. For instance, let us compare Wittgenstein's criterion of understanding 'Now I can go on', with a case of 'knowledge how', i.e., a skill. It would be odd indeed if someone, having understood the principle of a mathematical series, proceeded, correctly, to carry on the series without being able to say something, however inadequate, about what it is he understands. But where the performance counts as 'knowledge how', different considerations arise. In such cases I may know how to do something without being able to say what this knowledge consists in, beyond saying something like 'I *just* know' or, alternatively, by demonstrating the skill. Here it would not necessarily be odd if the person concerned could not say anything about how he knows; one can know something—how to do x—without knowing what that knowledge consists in.

These two cases differ in an essential respect: in the 'criterion of understanding' example, there is necessarily *some* propositional content expressible in words; whereas in the 'knowledge how' example this does not seem necessarily to be so. There is nothing which is necessarily expressible beyond the actual performance, which is, in this case, a sufficient condition for knowledge. I wish, therefore, to suggest that, where understanding is concerned, there is necessarily something propositional about it in a way which is not necessarily the case where knowledge is concerned. It has also been shown that we cannot simply substitute 'know' for 'understand' where the object is 'propositions'. Having said this, let us consider the role of proposition understanding in the wider context of the content of understanding.

1.2 Content of Understanding

While it is quite unequivocal to speak of understanding persons this is not the case when speaking of objects, e.g., 'I understand John' as opposed to 'I understand this table'. The two propositions highlight issues which are directly related to the notion of content of understanding. In the first proposition we are expressing something which is undoubtedly different from the second proposition which seems nonsensical—tables are not entities to be understood in the sense that people are. But in so far as certain objects possess individual idiosyncracies this feature may demand understanding of a particular object, i.e., a particular car, as distinct from the understanding of what cars are in general. We could supply a context to the notion of a particular object, involving certain of its properties, which could be understood in terms of what might be referred to as its 'behaviour'; why it 'responds' only to some specific person's handling or the particular treatment it 'needs'. The implication, however, is obvious; when speaking of understanding certain particular material objects we tend to speak in anthropomorphic terms. We endow objects with ways of behaviour usually reserved for persons; the more complex the object the more natural the transition. The crucial point is that, in supplying an explication of our understanding of a situation surrounding an object, we speak of what could be termed pseudo-action on the part of the object concerned; something that the object does/performs or fails to do/perform. This is, of course, a 'courtesy attribution' in so far as we do not attribute intentions in this context; but the attribution is, nevertheless, a valid one in so far as the complexities surrounding the given object involve something that is going on.

I said above that the understanding under discussion involves understanding complexities surrounding a particular object. I do not wish to suggest that such understanding applies exclusively to particular objects. We understand that objects, generally, may possess certain idiosyncracies. But the point at issue is that an object qualifies as a candidate for understanding on our part (as opposed to knowledge in the sense of acquaintance) only in cases where the particular set of complexities surrounding the particular object can be specified in propositional form. Thus whether we are prepared to speak in terms of knowing something or understanding it seems to be dependent on contextual considerations. Generally, understanding something, e.g., cars, involves a degree of complexity in the object and its surroundings which merely knowing what cars are does not; what we understand in the second case is a general principle of individuation which enables us to pick out cars in general. What is being understood in the first case are certain specific situations which apply to certain particular objects.

For our original proposition about the table to have sense there has to be something about the particular table, some situation which is statable in propositional form. Thus, in certain cases when we make the contrast between knowing x and understanding x, we stress the difference between knowing something simpliciter (having the concept of x and being able to pick out x) and understanding the situation surrounding that particular x.

The general notion of situation is one with which I shall concern myself throughout this book but at this stage, in summary, we need to see how, if at all, my account differs from Popper's.

In so far as Popper takes propositions and situations to be paradigmatic objects of understanding, he is undoubtedly right, as I have tried to show, particularly via my discussion of the content of understanding. But whereas Popper insists that objects of the third world have an existence independent of the knowing subject or the subject who created them, I shall argue that there is, necessarily, a distinction between scientific and psychological explanation of understanding and that, therefore, we cannot, contrary to Popper's assertion, employ the same methods in science and in the sphere of understanding persons and works of art.

Popper dismisses all areas of enquiry which do not lend themselves to his methodology on the grounds that these areas could not be seriously considered as candidates for knowledge and understanding of any objective kind whatsoever. I shall try to show how objective considerations can, and do, enter into my account of personal understanding and my discussion will implicitly draw further attention to the inadequacy of Popper's theory of understanding others and the self. My usage of 'situation' is closely tied to that of the notion of content of understanding. A situation which someone is trying to understand or claims to understand implies that person's participation in it, not merely to the extent that the situation imposes itself on the person concerned but, as importantly, that the given person contributes to the interpretation of the situation in his attempts to understand. It might be objected that this is not participation. I shall reserve further comment on this point till Chapter 2 where the issue will be discussed in detail.

Understanding each situation is an understanding of a content surrounding a given object or person. It is that content which has to be grasped by the intelligence, the understanding of the given person. How this is done cannot be specified in terms of some particular formula because there are different ways by which different persons come by understanding of the complexities involved in any situation. The process by which we both conceive a number of true propositions and affirm them to be true cannot be adequately represented by way of some fixed formula. I have, so far, separated knowledge in the sense of acquaintance from other kinds of knowledge such as demand understanding of contents statable in propositional form; understanding an object in a given situation. I have already tried to bring out the point that there is necessarily something propositional about understanding in a way which is *not* necessarily the case where certain kinds of knowledge are concerned. I now wish to extend this claim and shall attempt to argue that there is necessarily something propositional about understanding that makes situations paradigmatic subject matter of understanding in that what a situation involves can and must be seen in propositional terms.

It seems to me that we might approach this task by asking whether we could separate or specify items which form the particular subject matter of understanding within the realm of knowledge in general. We could, perhaps, begin by speaking generally in terms of objects qua objects of knowledge, and see how our understanding is engaged and what it focuses on in this context.

D. W. Hamlyn offers one way of discussing what objects of knowledge are in his paper, 'Person-perception and Our Understanding of Others'.[8] By way of introduction to the discussion, I quote a short passage from his book, *The Theory of Knowledge*:

Knowledge of anything demands an understanding of the kind of thing that the object of the knowledge is, and full knowledge requires full understanding. Part of what is involved in speaking in this way of 'the kind of thing that the object of the knowledge is' is the sort of relations it can have with us and we with it.[9]

Hamlyn goes on to explain this in the above-mentioned paper by setting up three principles which specify three necessary (though not sufficient) conditions of our being said to know x in terms of understanding such relations. He argues that for anything to count as an object of knowledge it must be something capable of standing in a relation to us and we to it.

Hamlyn divides objects of knowledge into various categories: material objects, facts, properties, persons. It is the category to which an object of knowledge belongs which to a large extent determines what sort of relationship we can be said to have with it. If it belongs to the category of facts then our relationship can be partly spelled out in terms of my attitude as to the truth or falsity of the given fact, my believing it, accepting or rejecting it and so on. If the object of knowledge belongs to the category of material things one of the possible relations in which I can stand towards it is that of user. People are also objects of knowledge but one of the distinctions between this category and the previous one is precisely that my relationship to other people cannot be always that of a user. To see people entirely as objects to be used is to labour under a grievous misconception as to what sort of things persons are. But here my relations with other persons cannot be specified because they will depend to a large extent on the sort of personal relationship I may establish with a given person.

Hamlyn's three principles which specify the necessary but not sufficient conditions of our being said to know x are:

1. That we should understand what kind of relation can exist between the object of knowledge and the person claiming to know it.
2. That, in addition, we must know through experience what is involved in standing in an appropriate relation to things of the kind that x is.
3. That we must actually stand to x in relations which are appropriate to the kind of thing that x is.

1. This Principle states that as a part of what is to count as our having a concept of x we must understand the sort of relation in which we can stand to this object as well as those in which we cannot stand.
2. This Principle demands knowledge of what is involved in

standing in an appropriate relation to things of the kind that x is, through experience. This demand implies knowledge obtained through having had experience of things of the kind that x is. It would, thus, be rather odd to claim that one had experience of standing in an appropriate relation to things of the kind that x is without actually having had experience of things of the kind that x is. In the case of claiming to know a particular person it is not enough, however, to have come to know through experience what it is to stand in an appropriate relation to people in general. Here an additional necessary condition is needed, that of actually standing in some relation to the person concerned.

This leads into Principle 3. A necessary condition of our being said to know x is that we must actually stand to x in relations which are appropriate to the kind of thing that x is. My understanding the appropriateness of a relationship to a given object depends on the correct conception of the thing in question. But, in addition to this, my understanding of a given object of knowledge is determined in many cases by the kind of role I play in relation to the object (but Hamlyn argues explicitly against the idea that an account of this issue could be given entirely in terms of roles). These roles differ. Thus my knowing my typewriter includes my understanding the relation in which I stand to it as a user. It also includes my knowing that the 'g' tends to stick and so on. But it need not include my knowing how to repair it when something goes wrong because that, strictly speaking, is not a part of what my role is; this is a part of the role played by, say, a mechanic. My understanding of what I can or cannot do with it is also a part of the relation in which I stand to it; I cannot, for instance, use it for practising scales on. Although I may get annoyed with it and hit it in my anger, I understand that this is not an appropriate thing to do to a typewriter because, for instance, it is incapable of responding to my treatment; it is an inanimate object.

In all these principles one point is brought out again and again—for me to claim to know a thing—a necessary but not a sufficient condition of my being said to know it is to be able to have certain relevant concepts and to understand certain things about the object of knowledge. Part of my understanding certain things about the object of knowledge is my understanding of the relations which can hold between me and the object of knowledge.

B

Thus, in order to know x we have to know the kind of relation which can hold between us and x; this in turn presupposes understanding the appropriate relation between me and the object of knowledge.

The relevance of Hamlyn's paper to our topic stems from his clear analysis of the role understanding plays in our claims to know an object. The understanding is engaged in large measure on *kinds* of relations; our claims to know what such relations are presuppose understanding what relations are appropriate. This important point leads us directly to our immediate concern. An object of knowledge is something in principle knowable and thus in principle understandable, but the resulting understanding may be qualitatively different on the part of various persons. This is because we come to understand contents surrounding given objects in different ways. On a certain level our understanding does not differ in this way and this is on the level of enabling us to identify x as a such and such; this is a part of our being able to actually know x or come to know x. Such understanding involves concepts and their application, not just objects in the world per se, although we can understand things qua instantiations of concepts. On this level, having the concept 'table', understanding of what sort of objects tables are, is presupposed in our ability to pick out tables as tables. But on a more complex level we do not merely form judgments of identification; we employ our understanding in a way which results in new or wider understanding: coming to understand unfamiliar relations and coming to understand situations surrounding objects of knowledge.

While anything which is the subject matter of understanding requires the application of various concepts, it necessarily possesses a complexity which objects of knowledge, qua objects of knowledge, do not necessarily possess. This point can also be brought out by the examples I have given. We understand persons, relations, theorems, situations and so on but we do not understand tables qua tables—what we understand here is what sort of things tables are. But tables, in common with other material objects such as cars, machines, works of art, can be understood in terms of situations and thus complexities surrounding them in as much as there *is* some situation, some content surrounding the object to be understood. Objects may or may not have a history which contributes to our being able to know them

as, e.g., the objects they are, i.e., identifying them and also knowing some things about them—propositional knowledge which
presupposes understanding. By contrast, the proposition 'I know
"red" but I don't understand it', is nonsense because we are
speaking here of the property 'red' qua property. The point is
that 'knowing red' could only mean 'being able to recognise it',
whereas knowing a particular car involves this plus knowing
something about it, understanding the situation with regard to it.
Persons, being complex objects, allow both particularly and in
every case the possibility (in principle) of being both known and
understood just because the necessary complexity is presupposed.
Hence our original statement: 'I understand John' has force.

1.3 Person Understanding

To know any person is to know him through acquaintance, by
confrontation and this involves also having the concept of persons,
understanding what sort of things persons are, what relations are
appropriate to the sort of things persons are and so on. In the
same respect, to know a material object, I may know it through
acquaintance or confrontation and this knowledge also involves
having the concept of that object, understanding what sort of
things such objects are, what relations are appropriate to the sort
of things they are and so on. In other words I can be said to know
Margaret Thatcher in just the same sense as I know my typewriter, i.e., I can recognise her and know a few things about her,
etc. But the respects in which I can know a person and a typewriter, listed above, involve very different considerations, e.g.,
considerations brought into play in understanding what relations
are appropriate to the kind of things persons are as opposed to
what relations are appropriate to typewriters. The kinds of
relations are different. The difference in kind is closely bound up
with the fact that these objects represent a different kind of case.
Once the relations, appropriate to the kind of things typewriters
are, have been understood, it is also understood that such relations
are largely applicable to all cases of knowing typewriters. This is
because relations to such machines are relatively simple; the scope
is limited. This is not the case where understanding what relations
are appropriate to the kind of things persons are, is concerned;
at least, not entirely the case. We understand what relations are

appropriate to the kind of thing persons are in general. But, in addition, we have to consider complications arising from the particular case. We stand in relations of various kinds to different individuals; these relations are governed by the roles in which the individuals stand to each other, attitudes that are taken up and so on. What may be an appropriate relation to one person may not be appropriate to another.

Further, understanding persons is rather different from understanding material objects in that each person is paradigmatically a candidate for understanding since the existence of intricate situations is implied by the sort of thing a person is. This is because we have prior knowledge, stemming from our understanding of the kind of things persons are in general, that each and every person is a complex object and therefore the understanding of such an object must necessarily be complex; thus a given content to be understood is guaranteed. No such guarantee can be extracted from our prior knowledge stemming from our concept of objects. Objects may or may not be taken as candidates for understanding (hence the proposition used in our example needs some further elucidation) but if persons are not so taken then, importantly, they are not seen as persons in the full sense. It is *the kind* of complexity that is important for understanding.

According to the psychiatrist Anthony Storr:

When we enter a new situation in life and are confronted by a new person, we bring with us prejudices of the past and our previous experiences of people. These prejudices we project upon the new person. Indeed, getting to know a person is largely a matter of withdrawing projections; of dispelling the smoke-screen of what we imagine he is like and replacing it with the reality of what he is actually like.[10]

Translating this into a philosophical context, I wish to argue that applying general concepts on meeting a particular person, i.e., concepts relating to the sort of things persons are, already implies seeing that person as a candidate for involved understanding. This, however, so far, carries no implications as to the extent to which we will succeed in understanding the particular person. Finding oneself in a new situation it is important not to apply prejudices stemming from our previous experience of people, not to apply what are commonly referred to as labels from a stock of such labels. To attempt this is to see a person as an object to which we apply generalised knowledge of what makes 'people tick' or trying to infer or deduce things about him. This is precisely Storr's point—that we bring in already established categories, etc., whereas getting to know and understand a person is largely a matter of withdrawing projections and dispelling the smoke-screen of what we imagine he is like.

Storr is not alone in holding this view. Recently a number of psychologists have expressed dissatisfaction with psychological classifications of persons by application of established categories. They see such procedures as trivial and artificial and, more importantly, as a source of embarrassment. The tendency is to establish procedures which would take account of the kind of issues which Storr raises. Liam Hudson, for instance, has recently made serious attempts to indicate new directions for psychological explanation, away from what he calls the self-consciously scientific psychology—an activity filled with the paraphernalia of false science and apparent objectivity. He points out that statistical theories, e.g., of intelligence, were constructed by men who, in many cases, '. . . eschewed all but the most marginal contacts with the creatures their theories were about.'[11] He is very critical of statistical methods, which he refers to as 'number crunching' and 'the ritual observance in Psychology', and argues forcibly that in order to avoid embarrassment of trivial and artificial explanations one has to view psychology as not exclusively a science but also as an important part of the humanities.

He writes:

My argument has been that as a cultural entity, psychology has had the misfortune to cut itself off both from its neighbours, and also, to an alarming extent, from the raw material out of which its own fabric should properly be built. Psychology should stretch continuously—as until quite recently it did stretch—from the creative and scholarly arts on the one hand, to the established sciences on the other; and it should overlap generously with both.[12]

He also expresses a fervent hope that, with luck,

. . . , the more mindless among the statistical analyses in which we are

now in danger of drowning will find no natural home at all. Recruit-
ment to the profession will begin to favour those whose technical
abilities are matched by perceptiveness in personal matters.[13]

Hudson sums up the problems facing psychological explanation
(echoing Storr) in a telling passage:

The special awkwardness of psychological interpretation is that our
concepts are general, but that the focal point of our interpretation
remains stubbornly particular: the individual. Sometimes, for the
limited purpose of a specific argument, one can get away with evidence
about people considered as a sample. But to believe that short-cuts
must be possible, and that the individual will evaporate if ignored, is
to inhabit cloud-cuckoo-land.[14]

Psychology students often feel very disillusioned with their
courses which don't fulfil their expectations of enabling them to
understand themselves and other persons better; they look for the
individual and the personal but find that psychology is concerned
with generalisations which are considered safer and more respectable. The difference between their expectations and their course
emphases could be summarised as the difference between 'evidence' and personal experience.

The above points raise important issues about psychological
explanation and are very relevant to our topic, particularly since
the tendency is to depart from scientific methodology in Popper's
sense and also because they focus on specific difficulties in our
areas of concern. The issues raised need some further explanation,
but space forces me to be very brief on a matter of formidable
complexity. I shall limit myself to that part of psychological
explanation which is concerned with predicting behaviour based
on some kind of understanding of individual persons and ignore
all other branches of psychology such as recent cognitive psychology, etc.

1.3(a) Psychological Explanation concerning Individual People

It is very significant that the above reactions to prevalent psychological methodology in the area of person understanding are not
new in the sense of only recently finding expression. They are the
result of profound, long-term disagreements among psychologists

of different schools about the efficacy of the various matrices, alluded to earlier, which are available to them. This is an all important issue in psychology since what personality theorists and clinical psychologists have to decide is whether a given approach really can help one to understand people better. What is significant is that the dispute is of such long standing.

Paul Meehl, for example, expresses a deep-felt unease about predictive methodology in his book published in 1958.

There is no convincing reason to assume that explicitly formalised mathematical rules and the clinician's creativity are equally suited for any given kind of task, or that their comparative effectiveness is the same for different tasks. Current clinical practice should be much more critically examined with this in mind than it has been.[15]

I shall use Meehl's discussion because it highlights an important distinction stemming from the same concerns which Storr and Hudson express and which is also directly relevant to our topic. He poses the question: How should one go about predicting how a person is going to behave? The major methodological problem is one of choice or relation between 'clinical' and 'statistical' methods of prediction.

Critics of the clinical method, which proceeds on the basis of interview impressions, data from the history of the individual, etc., tend to view it as mystical, vague, unreliable, intuitive and non-scientific. The statistical method aims at assigning an individual to a class or set of classes on the basis of objective facts about him, his psychometric test scores, behaviour ratings or check-lists. It is claimed that the combination of these data enables one to classify the subject; this classification then leads to checking statistical or actuarial tables which give statistical frequencies of behaviour of various sorts for persons belonging to the given class. The *mechanical* (my emphasis) combining of information for classification purposes results in empirically determined, relative frequency probability figures thus claiming scientific status. Psychologists opposed to this method criticise it on the grounds that, e.g.:

Such standardisation by its very nature ignores the individual. . . . All our theories of personality are at variance with the notion that the summation of a series of items determined by discrete frequency tables could ever be expected to give an accurate dynamic picture of the individual.[16]

Another telling criticism is that made by G. W. Allport:[17] 'If predictions based on frequency were all that were possible, then a Hollerith machine worked on the basis of known frequencies by a robot could predict future behaviour as well as a sensitive judge.'

Meehl expresses his unease about classifications by saying that when a person is in a state of respect (showing respect to someone) there is no *one* defining property of a set of responses by which we recognise a person in a state of respect which can be stated physicalistically; responses may co-vary in strength and yet have no common topography. Many clinicians today speak of the necessity for understanding the 'meaning' of a given segment of behaviour to the 'whole person'. In other words, we must understand something of the 'whole person' before we can begin to understand the significance of some of his specific behaviour, we have to understand the situation in which he finds himself and what that situation means to him. In contrast, actuarial (statistical) predictions could only work if assumptions about complete determinism turned out to be true. This is far from being the case. Meehl himself provides us with a very good example of the inadequacy of the statistical method, quite unintentionally. On p. 62 of his book he speaks of 'salesperson', while earlier in the book he refers to 'the uninspired actuarian/technician' as a she. We could form several hypotheses here, e.g., that he only pays lip-service to equality of the sexes, that he had a particular female technician in mind while writing, hence the slip, etc., etc. What would settle the question here? Certainly no amount of classification of the two 'pieces of behaviour' but one's personal knowledge and understanding of Meehl.

Meehl states, tellingly, that he fears that the formulating of complex hypotheses, of the kind which are demanded if one is sensitive to the uniqueness of individuals and their idiosyncratic needs, is only possible for the clinician 'if we reject a categorical analysis and recognise that we deal not with response and stimulus and need *classes* but rather with clusters, the elements of which differ on a whole set of dimensions . . .', then we need what Meehl calls the creative act which is possible only for the clinician. Clinicians don't claim to be dealing with patients who are *completely* unique and idiosyncratic, if by 'completely' is meant that there are no similarities between patients. They try, however, to see each patient as a patient who is an individual. Statisticians, on the other hand, equate the non-deductive or non-formal with the irrational. And here we collide head on with the familiar dilemmas of 'Art or Science?' and 'subjective versus objective' judgments.

The statistical method certainly links up with Popper's scientific method in so far as it attempts to deal exclusively with third-world objects independently of any one subject, whereas the clinical method is based on some kind of confrontation between two individuals: the clinician and the patient; it is in this sense personal, an approach which the former method precludes. I shall deal with this distinction in great detail in Chapter 3 but for the present some general remarks will prove useful.

The issue at stake is crystallised by Storr's point which is, in effect, a plea to stop categorising, classifying or labelling people; to replace a tendency to see people as objects to be sorted with an attempt to withdraw projections and see persons as unique individuals. The above discussion centres on two related problems. One is the vast problem of probability theory, the other focuses on the crucial question as to what the aims of psychology are. Let us therefore first look at a hypothetical situation in relation to the claims made by statisticians.

1.3(b) Understanding of Hypothetical Situations about People

Supposing I make the statement—'I know, in spite of appearances to the contrary, that John is unhappy'. It is open to the hearer to ask me how I know this and he must, in asking this question seriously, already have some idea as to what he would be prepared to accept as a satisfactory answer. In the same way, in answering him, I have to bear in mind what sort of answer is required of me. Thus a satisfactory answer to this question would be in terms of my understanding of the situation in which John finds himself and what it is about it that makes him unhappy, my pointing out that although he usually seems cheerful and in a good mood, this does not belie my claim to know that he is unhappy. I could go on to explain how certain remarks, taken in conjunction with others, led me to interpret them in such a way as to confirm my claim. In this case a fairly straightforward explanation is possible. But suppose we now change this example somewhat to—'If John had gone to the party he would have enjoyed himself.' This example is, perhaps, more interesting as it also raises the problem of counterfactual conditionals. I am not here concerned with law-governed counterfactual conditionals as they fall outside the scope of my example and of the problem raised in psychological explanation. I am concerned with what Hampshire calls the justification of historical counterfactuals, as distinct from scentific ones in that a law deductive model cannot be applied to historical explanation in the way it is applied to explanations in the sciences.[18]

Now, if we examine the counterfactual—'If John had gone to the party he would have enjoyed himself', we find that we cannot apply any Universals of Law at all. If we try to apply Universals of Fact of the kind—'All the people who were at the party enjoyed themselves', this does not help. What, then, takes place when we make such counterfactual statements? When we say—'If John had gone to the party he would have enjoyed himself', we take into account all sorts of considerations. These are to a large extent belief-governed. Any counterfactual involves a statement about an imaginary or hypothetical situation and yet the statement or description of the imaginary/hypothetical situation is based on non-imaginary considerations. The statement is based on inferences from something else relevant to the situation, something we know, believe or understand. A difficulty arises because our inferences cannot ever be completely valid as certain premises are missing. Thus we can, at best, produce only an incomplete argument for any counterfactual conditional. We can understand and also accept a counterfactual conditional without completing the argument; we can accept it by accepting reasons which are provided and which sustain the claim made.

Thus grounds or reasons which would sustain the counterfactual conditional—'If John had gone to the party he would have enjoyed himself', would be expressed as probabilities based on one's knowledge and understanding of John. The probability is that John would have enjoyed himself. My thinking this probable is based on my understanding of John, on my understanding that the sort of people who attended the party were of a kind he usually gets on with, my understanding what this involves. I may know that he received some good news and would be only too ready to enjoy himself; it is a good party and so on. But underlying this knowledge is my understanding of John the person and, therefore, of my understanding of how these facts would be likely to influence him. I call these latter considerations belief-governed, the belief being based on my understanding of John and of the relevance of the considerations as applying to John. I do not wish to say here that counterfactuals of this kind are, therefore, merely expressions of beliefs. They are belief-governed in the sense that, being incomplete arguments and thus 'partial inferences', they lack complete justification and, as such, cannot attain the status of knowledge. In counterfactual conditionals of this kind we shift from a supposition to the conclusion based on relevant understanding and beliefs but a gap necessarily remains. Thus, given all the above probabilities, based on my understanding of the kind of person John is, John may, for some reason unknown to me, be in a particularly morose mood at the relevant time, in which case he would not have enjoyed himself and this would, retrospectively, show that the shift from the supposition to the conclusion was erroneous in this case. The inferences or arguments I have put forward were bases for my asserting the counterfactual (in terms of high probability), not of logically deducing it as a conclusion (offering complete justification), since, per impossibile, not all the premises were given. My asserting the counterfactual was not an expression of knowledge.

The point is that we do use counterfactual conditionals in reasoned argument; we use them legitimately if we are justified in holding a set of beliefs which would sustain them, of having reasons for adhering to them. If counterfactual claims are not tied to some general claim sustained by a Universal of Law, then the conclusion is not justified by any law-like statement but there is still good reason for accepting counterfactuals, if they are based on judgments made on the strength of one's understanding of the hypothetical situation.

Although the situation itself is hypothetical or imaginary, in my example whether or not John would have enjoyed himself, not all the contributing factors are hypothetical or imaginary; a number of factors are based on and stem from one's understanding of

John. It is this understanding which makes possible any judgments we make and this applies, it seems to me, to counterfactuals of this kind. This example, like the previous ones, focuses on the close relationship between knowledge and understanding, with particular reference to the importance understanding plays in cases where, although we can make inferences based on our understanding of John, understanding John does not always entail knowledge.

In the above discussion we were concerned with the role understanding plays in certain kinds of judgments, understanding which is brought to bear on a hypothetical situation; we also saw, to some extent, what sort of considerations the understanding focused on. The most important point which emerges against statistical methods of psychological prediction is that, in my example, the predictive statement is based on the speaker's *previous* knowledge and understanding of John, on their previous and ongoing relationship, a factor which is absent in the scientific methodology of statistical psychology. The second, related, problem, that of the aims of psychology, is too vast, and outside our immediate concerns, to discuss specifically. The distinction which *is* relevant is that between kinds of understanding and purposes from which our wishing to understand stem. It is this issue which focuses on our primary concern throughout the book.

To understand a person is, as I shall argue, inseparable from understanding something of his relationships with others. Responses to questionnaires will not yield any adequate information in that area for several reasons; how a person interprets his own responses is not necessarily incorrigible. If he is a patient then, by definition, he is disturbed in some way and his answers may be unreliable. The procedures lack the objective test of a person's responses in situations with other people.

Paradoxically, we must allow for the fact that some patients and their clinical-analysts cannot establish the necessary rapport with each other, that there are combinations of personal traits in certain clinicians which render them inept at some kinds of clinical activity. If we do not allow for this then we must allow the possibility of an infinite plasticity on the part of adult human beings to adopt any kind of personality trait they deem necessary in given circumstances. But if this were the case then categorising and classifying would prove impossible indeed.

The crux of the matter is to be clear about what we are categorising or classifying for, what are our purposes? In so far as concepts (universals) have a number of particular instantiations then classifying or categorising any particular presents no problems beyond fairly straightforward identification; in the case of persons, the exercise amounts to listing and categorising/classifying a certain number of observable attributes, ranging from the colour of hair to classifications into the category of 'shy', 'introvert', etc. The difficulties arise when we try to find out the reasons for the particular attribute, the experiences in the history of the individual which contributed to it and so on. It is in this area that psychologists find serious inadequacies in the prevalent methodology. (Hence the feelings of unease expressed by Meehl, et al.)

Meehl concludes by saying that having devoted so much time to a discussion of how the clinician's approach *could* transcend the limitations of the statistical method, ultimately, however, he is forced to accept that there is no evidence of the former method's superiority. Ultimately, as he puts it, we might as well face it, the shadow of the statistician hovers in the background; always the actuary will have the final word. This is because the validity of a clinician's claims will have to be established by an acceptable validation study. Meehl assumes that the only acceptable method of validation is the statistical method, the very assumption which Hudson seriously questions. Nevertheless, Meehl recognises that there is something important to be said for the personal, or what he calls 'creative', approach of the clinician but is unable to spell out what the important element, which enables real understanding to take place, consists of. This is the task I have set myself.

One of the characteristics of understanding persons, understanding which results in some knowledge of that person, is that much of such knowledge is not transferable to another person in a way in which we can and do transfer previous knowledge in cases of individuation of things. A part of what we understand of a given person is a part of the Gestalt of that person. It is true that once we have the concept 'person' we are able correctly to pick out persons. But much of the understanding we have of a given person does not carry any implications as to whether we can transfer this understanding and knowledge to another person.

We have to see each person as a person with his own particular complexities; our understanding is focused not so much on issues about what makes people tick in general but what the person concerned is 'telling' us of himself; we have to learn what he in particular is actually like. This involves being aware that there may be aspects of the new situation which are quite outside our past experiences with persons in general and which will, therefore, require an effort at new understanding. Seeing another as a candidate for understanding involves employing one's understanding in judgments as to what does and does not apply to a particular person. We bring our understanding to bear on judging what, and to what extent, we can extract from our general experience and knowledge of persons and what it is appropriate to apply in a particular case. But this judgment is based on and, as it were, dictated by the person we are trying to understand. Our understanding here is bound up with highly selective judgments and a real effort to curb jumping to hasty conclusions. An important part of what it is to understand someone is that one is constantly aware of any change in them and sensitive to the possibility of such changes occurring. That is one reason why Storr's point has force and significance as part of our preliminary discussion of how we apply existing knowledge to things, and difficulties about such application to persons.

1.4 Persons in Situations

As I said at the beginning, it depends to a very large extent on our particular interests and our capacities what aspects of a situation we are capable of understanding. This point is particularly relevant to understanding persons in situations. Some people seem to have a far greater ability than others for understanding persons and thus an ability for personal relationships. This is, it seems to me, due partly to the degree of interest one has in others but it cannot be the whole story. It was once said to me that perhaps people who have this ability to understand others well possess certain extra concepts which not everyone has. This suggestion *as it stands*, seems to me, ex hypothesi, impossible to evaluate. If I lack these concepts then there is nothing I can say about them; if, on the other hand, I do possess certain of these concepts, I may be entirely unaware that I am applying them where others could not do so. The suggestion, then, seems rather problematic as I cannot think what such concepts would be like. I shall discuss this point again in Chapter 2. For the present I would suggest that the problem is, perhaps, analogous with that which applies to reading a complex novel—some people will understand it better than others in that they will 'get more out of it', will not miss the finer nuances, or they may even disagree in their interpretations. It seems to me that this may not be in any way dependent on having certain concepts over and above those of other readers (given that the words of the novel are understood by all), but rather on a way of approaching the novel. This needs unpacking—I mean here something like Hamlyn's Principle B mentioned above. In one sense one cannot, of course, have the sort of relationship Hamlyn talks about with a fictional situation but a description of this fictional situation may be analogous with one which we have come to understand through our own actual experience and we are therefore in a better position to understand what the author may be trying to say.

Another way of explaining what I mean may be as follows: Saying that I have a similar pain to that of another person does not commit me to saying that I can only understand statements about the feelings of others in terms of my own experience. My own experience may not help very much. But I think that someone who has suffered much pain may somehow be more understanding of other sufferers, although, of course, he may quite easily be the opposite. The point is that he is in a position to be more understanding. He may have a fellow feeling and this possibility involves the idea of open-ended concepts, concepts which admit of further development, in this case through experience. But I do not think that this is the same as saying that one has new concepts which others, somehow, have not got.

The distinction I am trying to make can be brought out by a quotation from Goethe's poem 'Dieselbe':

> Only he understands how I feel
> who has experienced longing.[19]

The point is not that I am incapable of understanding what longing is unless I myself have experienced it but that by experiencing it my concept of what longing is becomes much richer and I am, therefore, in a position to understand it to a greater degree than before. Malcolm, in his memoir of Wittgenstein, writes describing the last hours of Wittgenstein's life:

'Tell them I've had a wonderful life!' By 'them' he undoubtedly meant his close friends. When I think of his profound pessimism, the intensity of his mental and moral suffering . . . , I am inclined to believe that his life was fiercely unhappy. Yet at the end he himself exclaimed that it had been 'wonderful'! To me this seems a mysterious and strangely moving utterance.[20]

This quotation seems to raise a problem. Malcolm found it strange and was unable to understand Wittgenstein's utterance, calling it 'mysterious'. It seems to me that in order to understand the worthwhile feeling and importance of one's pursuit at whatever cost we need more than an understanding of the rules governing the words used. It can only be understood by someone who understands the sort of work which brings happiness. We must understand, at least up to a point, what sort of happiness could be brought about by a given thing. We may think a particular way of life a complete waste, but as long as we understand how someone could be happy with it, we understand the feeling of the man concerned. Here, it seems, a different sort of understanding is required than in the case of pain, where some sort of understanding seems always possible. Yet many people would completely fail to understand Wittgenstein's remark. In such a case our own experience would be very significantly of help, more significantly than in the case of pain.

In knowing and understanding a situation we come to know and understand many aspects, or elements. The factual, objective description of a situation remains uniform in that it is quite independent of factors which influence *kinds* of possible, further and more complex, understanding and knowledge. The distinction here is between what there is for everyone to know and understand and what is understandable only from a certain point of view, within a person's limits. Knowledge is, and has to be, by its essence, objective. Our claiming to know and understand a situation on a certain level is claiming to know and understand factual, objective elements which constitute a description of what took place and which are quite independent of personal considerations. Further knowledge and understanding become selective according to one's interests, capabilities, etc. These subjective elements regulate what we come to know and how much we know. Our understanding, the quality and mode of our understanding, how we understand, is strongly ruled by subjective/personal considerations although based on objective knowledge. We may arrive at particular knowledge in different ways. Knowledge and understanding work in close concatenation both in the factual, objective descriptions of what took place and in cases where knowledge and understanding become selective and very dependent on personal considerations. Furthermore, there is a conceptual relation between the two concepts in that not only would we not have the concept of knowledge without that of understanding (and vice versa) but also in order to apply the one concept to anything it must be possible also to apply the other in some way.

But, at the same time, knowing something does not always entail understanding it, (it does not do so in some cases of knowledge through acquaintance or knowledge which is demonstrated in some skills), whereas understanding something does imply knowing it *in some way*. This is because not all kinds of knowledge possess propositional content whereas there is something essentially propositional about understanding in that we cannot understand something without understanding something about it. To put it differently, the propositional nature of understanding follows from the fact that what can be understood is *normally* expressible in words.

A part of what is involved in knowing x is an understanding of the appropriate relation in which I can stand to that object. Those and other relations may also constitute the subject matter of understanding. Situations qualify particularly as paradigmatic subject matter of understanding. In addition, as I have tried to argue throughout this chapter, there is necessarily something propositional about understanding which makes situations paradigmatic objects of understanding in that what a situation involves can and must be seen in propositional terms. The situation provides the complexity surrounding the object of knowledge.

In approaching any given situation, we bring to it our personal past knowledge and understanding, our personal mind's directedness towards what is to be understood. Our understanding, how we understand a given situation, will be based on our having been exposed to things/experiences in the past. This forms a vital link between personal experience and personal understanding. As Tolstoy noted, those who are accustomed to solitary, independent thinking do not easily grasp another's thought and are very partial to their own; but people in close contact with others apprehend one another's complicated meanings by 'laconic and clear' communication in the fewest words. This observation stresses the importance to personal understanding of the kind of things within a person's scope of knowledge—what kind of things fall within his experience. Personal understanding is determined by subjective life situations, hence we get such a variety of abilities and approaches to selective aspects of understanding. Objective knowledge is not so limited as it is not necessarily bound up with subjective experiences, as my quotation from Goethe shows. Gombrich, for instance, stresses that the way we see and depict things depends upon and varies with experience, practices, interests and attitudes.[21] These are things which a person has developed through personal contacts and which determine his personal understanding. I shall now discuss these personal elements in detail.

Notes

1 W. Shakespeare, *King Lear*, Act III, Scene VI, L. 75.
2 K. R. Popper, *Objective Knowledge*, Oxford, 1972, p. 106.
3 *Ibid.* p. 163.
4 *Ibid.* p. 167.
5 *Ibid.* p. 114.
6 *Ibid.* p. 179.
7 Aristotle, *De Anima*, Bk. 3, Chap. 3, 427a17 (Clarendon Aristotle Series, ed. J. L. Ackrill, 1968).
8 D. W. Hamlyn, 'Person-perception and Our Understanding of Others', in *Understanding Other Persons*, ed. T. Mischel, Basil Blackwell, Oxford, 1974.
9 D. W. Hamlyn, *The Theory of Knowledge*, Doubleday & Co., New York and Macmillan, London, 1970, p. 247.
10 A. Storr, *The Observer*, 12 July 1970.
11 L. Hudson, *The Cult of the Fact*, Jonathan Cape, 1972, p. 152.
12 *Ibid.* p. 157.
13 *Ibid.* p. 167.
14 L. Hudson, *Human Beings*, Paladin, 1978, p. 37.
15 P. E. Meehl, *Clinical versus Statistical Prediction*, University of Minnesota Press, Minneapolis, 1958, p. vi (preface).
16 R. Munroe, 'An Experiment in Large Scale Testing by a Modification of the Rorschach Method', *Journal of Psychology*, 13 (1942): 229-63.
17 G. W. Allport, 'The Use of Personal Documents in Psychological Science', *S.S.R.C. Bulletin*, No. 49 (1942), p. 159.
18 S. Hampshire, 'Subjunctive Conditionals', in *Analysis*, 1948.

19 Goethe, 'Dieselbe', in *Goethe's Poems*, ed. C. W. Eastman, Appleton-Century-Crofts Inc., New York, 1941, p. 47.
20 N. Malcolm, *Ludwig Wittgenstein—A Memoir*, Oxford University Press, 1958, p. 100.
21 E. Gombrich, *Art and Illusion*, New York, 1960.

2 *Personal Understanding*

2.1 Concepts and Understanding; Objective and Subjective Considerations

As Geach points out: 'Concepts are capacities exercised in acts of judgment . . .'.[1] It could be, and indeed has been, suggested that someone has the concept of x if he is able to use the word 'x' and this is equated with understanding the word 'x'. If this were so, it would be true to say that we have as many concepts as we have words. This seems odd. Understanding involves having concepts as well as understanding the relation between them. Many words perform the function of relating or linking; it would be odd to speak here of having the concept of 'it', 'thus', 'and' and so on. We understand the function these words perform, and we may or may not always have the concept of the grammatical categories to which they belong. It does not follow that it is right to speak of concepts corresponding to these words.

If we are asked what it is for someone to have the concept of a table, on the other hand, we should know what sort of answer would be acceptable, although this is not to say that our expectations would be tied to notions of an invariable set of necessary and sufficient conditions. We need merely to give an account and we know what sort of account would be acceptable. The paradigm here is that the person claiming to have the concept 'table' knows how to go on. He can pick out tables when he sees them and pick them out for the right reasons, etc. But one must bear in mind things such as values of x where it is not easily said what is involved in having a concept of them. Let us take x here as an ethical term. If we speak of someone having moral concepts we are implying that he knows what 'good' is, or 'justice' or 'duty'. And, as I take Socrates to have shown, this kind of knowledge cannot be stated in terms of any definitions.

Instead, I wish to suggest, the role concepts play here is linked closely to what we term a 'moral sense' which differentiates most of us from animals. The moral sense enables us to see situations arising *as* situations where an ethical judgment or decision or

38

action is called for and this involves understanding the issues pertinent to the particular case; seeing the context as a moral context. The part understanding plays here is directly related to understanding a given situation and seeing it as a situation of a certain kind, a context calling for a moral judgment. Thus there are difficulties about what is involved in having a concept as soon as we leave the realm of the purely descriptive.

An added complication is that a person may be said to have the concept of x to a greater or lesser extent, he may have a full or a partial concept of x. Some xs lend themselves to our speaking in terms of having a full concept of them, others do not. The issue becomes vastly complex when we ask, for instance, what it is for someone to have the concept of a disease. A schoolboy may have a partial concept of it but by saying this we must not jump to the conclusion that only a doctor could have the full concept. It would depend on whether he also had experience of it. A doctor's conception of any given disease is qualitatively different from that of a layman; his concept cannot be separated from the science of medicine itself. Thus the layman's concept is discussable in terms of our common understanding, that of a doctor in terms of the science of medicine. The fact that the doctor's understanding is a better understanding does not, I think, prejudice my point that it is not ipso facto complete understanding. Furthermore, supposing the schoolboy has suffered from a particular, perhaps rare, disease—he might get an insight into what the disease is like and so on, which the doctor may be quite unaware or ignorant of. I am not sure whether we could still claim that the doctor's understanding was better—only that it was different.

My point is, if I am right, that it is mistaken to ask 'What is it for someone to have the concept x?', if some specific kind of answer is expected, i.e., a uniform answer for all cases. This is because the question admits of a variety of answers; concepts are acquired in all kinds of ways. Who it is that has the concept is also highly relevant to the sort of answer we may expect. Concepts are kinds of objects of understanding but our operations with them also involve our understanding of relationships between them. What our individual claims to understanding or having given concepts amount to is closely tied to specific situations in which such claims are made.

Thus our acts of judgment depend on our understanding of a

given situation and the understanding we bring to it is dependent on the sort of connections we can make between what is known and has been learned by us with new knowledge and new learning. What I mean is that it makes no sense to speak of the possibility of someone's learning something or coming to understand something in isolation from what is already known by the particular person, i.e., unconnected with *his* previous understanding, as this would be the kind of 'learning' done by a parrot.

I shall call this the Principle of Personal Unity of Understanding which distinguishes one's personal, subjectively tinged understanding from general human understanding which is spelled out in general objective terms, and also from the product of animal learning. Each person's understanding is dependent on and built upon previous knowledge and understanding. But the extent and kind of understanding depends very much on any given person's limitations, interests and experiences and, therefore, the understanding which any one person brings to bear on a situation will differ from any other to some extent.

It is important to note, however, that any knowledge or understanding which one comes by must be knowledge and understanding of our world, within a common framework of understanding, that is, objective understanding from which our criteria of correctness stem, and this is based on the all important notion of agreements in our judgments.

Thus, however much one's understanding may be subjectively tinged, it has to fit within the common framework of understanding and agreement in judgments. Criteria of truth presuppose agreement in judgments. This point can be illustrated by Wittgenstein's remark in the *Philosophical Investigations* 241:

'So you are saying that human agreement decides what is true and what is false?'—It is what human beings *say* that is true and false; and they agree in the *language* they use. That is not agreement in opinions but in form of life.

Agreement in judgments is what makes objectivity possible although agreement cannot be equated with truth. Agreement in judgments is a necessary link, or bridge, as it were, between truth and our understanding within a given form of life. What is also important is that within this framework there is also room for disagreement as well as areas of discourse such as ethics, aesthetics, politics, where truth as such is very elusive even if agreement is possible, at least in principle. That there are many kinds or species of understanding no one would dispute, but it seems to me that deciding whether something has been understood has to be judged in terms of what holds in a given context rather than speaking generally, in terms of necessary conditions which override all contexts.

These considerations apply to anything which can intelligibly be spoken about, identified or discriminated. For instance, I can come to know that a person is dark, handsome and six feet tall, or ugly, or in love, or in pain, or walks slowly or quickly, is pleasant, arrogant, clever, easy to talk to, that this flower smells sweetly or that the cat just scratched me, and so on. In other words the fact that I can attribute certain predicates to a person or make certain judgments or discriminations depends on the publicity of these concepts arising from our form of life and the possibility of agreement in judgments. Some of these attributes can be seen, others may not be. But, and this for my purposes is an all important 'but', we need to focus our attention, in this context, on the subjective elements which influence our understanding.

The subjective elements direct and influence *the mode* of our understanding and it is essential for our understanding of others that we come to understand something of that personal mode in the other. This does not amount merely to a consideration of the other's point of view, i.e., taking into account that his understanding and what matters to him is determined by his point of view; this is only a part of what is involved. His mode of understanding is also determined by his particular limitations, points of reference and experiences which enrich his understanding of particular, given things, situations, etc. This needs spelling out.

Language and concepts are necessary to the possibility of our understanding the world. What has already been said about the necessary common framework of understanding and what this involves, shows the necessity of the publicity of concepts stemming from language. But equally, we need to stress phenomenological aspects of understanding in that each person has personal limits of knowledge and understanding. What a given person knows and understands is normally what he can express and understand by means of language. A person's language is also subject to his personal limitations though, nevertheless, very much a part of the language we use generally and in which we agree; the subjective elements which influence our understanding stem from and fit into the objective framework. Thus, what a given person cannot think, he cannot speak of or understand.

This point applies generally, but one particular person's limits differ from another's. What I have said so far is closely tied to the Wittgensteinian notion that the limits of a person's world are determined by language. But, it seems to me, an important qualification is needed. We must not take 'language' too strictly in this context. If we take it as referring exclusively to spoken language then, I think, certain difficulties arise. Are the limits of a person's world, of his understanding, entirely dependent on what he can say or what he can understand of what is said to him?

People communicate in all sorts of ways without words—by looks and by acting in certain ways—and although this can be seen as an extension of language, as a language without words, it is not language in the limited sense. Presupposed in this, however, is the necessary condition that all such communication must in principle be translatable into words (propositions). This leaves open the question what is to count as adequate for understanding here. I may have certain experiences which I may be hard put to express in words adequately enough for someone else to understand the experience I am describing. My explanation of what I understand in the experiences is only as good or as adequate as my command of my language, but does this necessarily mean that language, therefore, limits the understanding of my world? I do not think so because my experience, however vague its description, may be very meaningful to me and may add to my understanding.

Given these qualifications, it must be pointed out, however, that the meaningfulness of any experience is dependent on my understanding a language or, to put it more accurately, on my being a language user/speaker. In placing the dependence of any such understanding on language, I wish to make the point that any experience, as an isolated phenomenon, presupposes language on which depends a person's view of the world. This is because one's understanding of such experiences can only take place within a framework of concepts, within a complex background of our form of life. Any such experience, in so far as it is that of an adult human being, however vague, would be qualitatively *different* when experienced by a language user as opposed to, say, that experienced by an animal. It belongs to, fits into and forms a part of a different view of the world; this is not a matter of choice on our part because we cannot step outside such a framework. What a person knows and understands is paradigmatically what he can express and understand by means of language. The extent of a given person's knowledge of the world is dependent precisely on the extent of his being able to understand the world in understanding the sense of what is said about the world. *His* world is very much the objective world, everybody's world but limited by his personal limits. The subjective elements which thus influence our understanding stem from and fit into the objective framework. Any acts of judgment which we perform in, for example, deciding how to act in a given situation, are dependent on *our* particular understanding of it.

It needs to be stressed that knowledge is, and must be, by its essence, objective but the subjective or personal elements which enter into our attempts to know and understand anything cannot be ignored. These elements influence our selection of *what* we come to know and *how much* we know. The quality of our understanding, how we understand, what we understand, is strongly ruled by subjective/personal considerations although based on objective understanding.

2.2 Understanding, Perception and the Notion of Situation

In the previous chapter I discussed what is involved in understanding a situation and I argued that situations qualify particularly as objects of understanding. I want to go on to examine the notion of 'situation' as regards its importance for the concept of understanding. I shall try to extend the notion of situation to specific fields in order to see whether all understanding can be seen as understanding a situation or, in other words, whether an account of the concept of understanding can be given in terms of situations. For instance, I wish to suggest that understanding a work of art involves understanding a situation. To illustrate this we could, perhaps, ask to what extent our understanding of, say, a musical work depends on our capacity to extract not only from the work but also from our own experience. I wish to ask whether it is just a matter of reporting our feelings, explaining what our reactions are on contemplating a complex structure and content which are immediately objective or, whether it is *not* just the case that everything that is relevant to the understanding of a musical work is merely the objective character of the work. Is it perhaps the case that in some way we extract from our own experience a great deal which illuminates our understanding? If so, then it seems to me, our understanding here is also dependent to a large extent on the sort of person we are, just as I tried to show this with regard to understanding a situation. In other words, both in understanding a situation and a musical work, two kinds of understanding are involved—the objective and the personal. How far can this comparison be carried?

As I mentioned before, certain aspects of a situation are fairly straightforward and unambiguous. To use my previous example— the situation discussed can be stated quite simply: 'Valjean stole a loaf of bread'. Similarly we can state: 'He listened to a sonata'. Presupposed in both cases is the understanding of the concepts involved and just as in the case of stealing one has to understand a complex set of background concepts such as legal institutions, punishment, wrong or the society's structure as regards certain behaviour, so in the case of the sonata in order to identify it as such one has to have a knowledge of its structure. What counts as a sonata (e.g. in its classical form) is that it is written for one or two instruments, that it usually consists of three or four movements, one of which is usually written as a trio and one a slow movement. One has to be able to differentiate it from, say, a scherzo, a prelude, a symphony. To what extent one understands this will be dependent not only on the concepts one has but on knowledge of their correct application. The more of the factual background one understands in both examples, for instance, why an otherwise honest man stole a loaf and, in the second case, what key the sonata is in, what kind of modulations are used and so on, the more one becomes further acquainted with purely objective aspects of the situation. Our understanding of them depends on our ability to extract knowledge, to make ourselves acquainted with more data which can be analysed and is there for anyone to understand (at any rate, anyone who has the necessary background knowledge). If I do not know what a modulation is I will not recognise it as such in the work (although I may be aware, to some extent, of a change of key or mood), nor will I be in a position to understand why an otherwise honest man stole a loaf of bread if I do not know that he is otherwise honest; I will not be in a position to ask myself these questions.

On a more complex level, part of what is involved in the understanding of both my examples is the understanding necessary for making value judgments. In the first case this may be something about the competence with which Valjean stole; this might enable one to judge whether he was a habitual thief or a 'first offender'. In the case of listening to a sonata we may make judgments about the aesthetic value of the work or, perhaps, admire what we take to be very skilful handling of a beautiful theme followed by a masterly development. We may, in some cases, judge the composition an excellent example of the composer's technical merit and yet deny that the work has aesthetic value, i.e., we may judge it as a clever exercise in composition lacking artistic merit. And at the point where value judgments come in we enter into that aspect of the situation where our personal understanding becomes relevant.

I said in the previous chapter that in approaching any given situation we bring to it our personal past knowledge and understanding; our personal mind's directedness towards objects of understanding. Our personal understanding is determined by subjective life situations which give rise to varieties of ability and approach to selective aspects of understanding. I called the connection between the understanding and things (experiences) a person has been exposed to in the past the Principle of Personal Unity of Understanding (see p. 40). I shall attempt to elucidate this notion in detail and I wish, therefore, in this chapter, to concentrate entirely on the kind of understanding at stake here, understanding which to a large extent is dependent on the sort of person we are. To bring this point out I shall concentrate on Merleau-Ponty's *Le Visible et l'invisible*, part 2.[2] I have also used his article 'L'Oeil et l'esprit' as additional background.[3]

In a footnote to 'L'Oeil et l'esprit' the translator remarks on *Le Visible et l'invisible:*

'L'Oeil et l'esprit' was the last work Merleau-Ponty saw published. . . . According to Prof. Claude Lefort, 'L'Oeil et l'esprit' is a preliminary statement of ideas that were to be developed in the second part of the book Merleau-Ponty was writing at the time of his death— *Le Visible et l'invisible* (part of which was published posthumously by Gallimard in February, 1964).[4]

The passages I shall refer to are in the chapter entitled 'L'entrelace—Le Chiasme' (pp. 172-204 of the above edition). This chapter and the following short chapter 'Annexe' represent the second part referred to above.

It is essential, I think, to make as clear as possible to what extent I am prepared to go along with Merleau-Ponty. Firstly, this brand of continental philosophy uses a terminology which can be extremely misleading as it endows, or appears to endow, what is said with a kind of mystique for the non-practitioner. I shall, therefore, try to extract what I consider relevant and make what might prove a foolhardy attempt to put some of the terminology into more manageable language or to clarify it by examples. Secondly, there are certain difficulties in Merleau-Ponty's account which I shall discuss rather briefly as these do not really enter into my topic. I have chosen Merleau-Ponty mainly because of his discussion of the example taken from Proust's *Du Côté de Chez Swann*, part 2. This example serves to bring out very important aspects of the kind of personal understanding with which I am particularly concerned.

While not directly concerned with Merleau-Ponty's full-blown theory of perception, nor offering it merely as a background, I do find some parts of it suggestive. His approach seems to be more sensitive than that of other philosophers who have similar things to say. He stresses the importance of the relation between the perceiver and the perceived, offering very important insights and making significant distinctions. My purpose is to extract what is particularly relevant to our concerns, to build on it and develop my own account of personal understanding, particularly with the aid of the example referred to above.

In order to do this, an exegesis of the whole chapter is essential, as it is also essential to the understanding of the example. I must confess my reluctance to set out on an exegesis of something as obscure as this particular chapter but perhaps the effort and accompanying risks are justified for the reasons given.

2.2(a) The Phenomenology of Perception

A colour, Merleau-Ponty says, or any other visible in the world is not simply something existing by itself and offering itself to the seer, nor is there first a seer who is somehow empty and receives into himself that which he sees; in other words a visible is not simply offered to a merely receptive being. The colour or any other visible is that which is thought of as a sort of connective tissue between exterior and interior horizons, the horizons of the visible and the invisible.

This terminology will, I hope, become clearer presently. When we see a colour, it is not *that* colour per se which we see but a bridge between the visible and invisible worlds. The particular red seen emerges for us from a more general redness which first captures our gaze; only then do we fix our gaze and pick out this particular red from a 'background' of redness. As we perceive or apprehend it, it becomes bound up with texture (woolly, metallic or porous) and its colour is also relative to the colours which surround it. As Merleau-Ponty puts it: 'this red is what it is only by connecting up from its place with other reds about it, with which it forms a constellation.'[5]

This may be a case of attraction or repulsion but it is always a relation. A red dress, for instance, has its fibres stretched out with the fabric of the visible environment. A red dress appears to us against a background of red things: red tiles, red carpets, red pillar boxes or the red of certain terrains of Aix or Madagascar. It may appear against a field of red garments—military, judicial, regal, professorial. It is also seen against other red things—the communist flag or the red of a woman's hair. Merleau-Ponty also speaks of reds as fossils drawn from the depths of imaginary worlds, for example, the red of St. Nicholas' robe. In our particular seeing these fields are controlled or structured, the particular red reverberates, as it were, on heterogeneous red things, some nearer forming the backdrop, some further off conjured from our experience, but all within the interior and exterior horizons. The colour as a pure quality is an abstraction, not anything perceivable. We can never perceive what Merleau-Ponty calls 'a hard, naked chunk of being'; it is rather a 'sort of straits' between exterior and interior horizons ever open, flexible—it is less a colour or a thing, more a difference between things and colours, a momentary visibility of coloured being. The given colour is, as it were, enveloped, lived, sustained and nourished by a tissue which is not itself a thing but 'a flesh of things'.

This, I think, is a very sophisticated account of perception and if I understand Merleau-Ponty correctly, he does not mean that we are aware of all the above associations explicitly, in some sort of sequence, however rapid the succession. He says rather that all sorts of things in the exterior and interior worlds are related to the particular perception and what is more, are included in it. Some may be presented explicitly in thinking or in imagining. What is involved in this sort of awareness cannot be stated for all cases of perception because what Merleau-Ponty calls 'the ephemerical modulation of the visible' involves indefinite possibilities of variations, but if we think of perception as involving a sort of clustering of relevant things of which we may have a half-explicit or partly explicit awareness, a sensing of their proximity on the horizon, their potential as actual themes of consciousness, while others may remain in the background, this perhaps gives a clearer picture of what is at stake here.

Another naive example may serve to elucidate this further. At a conference, which I attended, I saw a mauve chalk mark on the blackboard which gave me a feeling of some vague, particular mauve something, but I could not think what caused this peculiar feeling though I was sure of some pleasurable connection with some other far off visible. It was not simply the mauve on the blackboard which I was perceiving. I did not succeed in consciously or explicitly identifying what it was that this particular mauve 'tried' to conjure up for me. This is a most incomplete way of illustrating a very involved point but it may serve as a mere indication.

Merleau-Ponty says that our glance is intimate with the visible things; it envelops and espouses them, it feels them. But it is not a question of manipulating them nor being utterly subservient to them. One cannot say simply whether it is the look which commands the things or the things the look. But in our perceiving a thing, the thing is in a relation with the look, it is as if we knew it before we started to get to know it, as if there were some pre-established harmony between us and the visible. Seeing, says Merleau-Ponty, is an inspired exegesis, an art of interrogating the visible according to its own wishes. This point is crucial. To return to my original concern—in listening to a piece of music I do not just perceive sounds but the music has a power, a power which is in the 'object' to invade our experience, provide experiences and connect with our past experiences all of which form the flesh of the visible, in this case audible.

It must be pointed out that Merleau-Ponty finds some difficulty with the audible. I shall return to this presently. He does, however, examine touch at great length and this may serve to illuminate the previous discussion of the visible. He asks how I give my hands the rate and diversion of movement whereby they enable me to feel the smooth and the rough. He argues that there must be some relation between what I do—the fairly rapid rotation of the fingers (this constitutes my exploration), and what it delivers to me or introduces me into—namely a tactile world. This can only happen if my hand is itself part of the tangible world, if it is one with things which touch or are touched. It is this intertwining of the tangible and the touching, the hand as part of both, which enables me to interrogate the universe of which my hand is a part. This could be interpreted as meaning that in touching, we are not only aware of the object we are touching, that is perceiving its texture and so on, but also, and as importantly, of the object touching us. I do not think that Merleau-Ponty actually makes this point but he does say:

. . . my hand, while it is felt from within, is also accessible from without, itself tangible, for my other hand, for example, if it takes its place among the things it touches, is in a sense one of them, opens finally upon a tangible being of which it is also a part. Through this crisscrossing within it of the touching and the tangible, its own movements incorporate themselves into the universe they interrogate, are recorded on the same map as it. . . .[6]

Through touch, then, we are aware simultaneously of the object being touched and of the touching by the touching hand. Merleau-Ponty's main point is that our having a sense of touch presupposes our being touchable, our being a tangible existent. He points out that similarly, having the sense of vision involves being visible; vision is in that sense analogous with touch.

I think there is a serious difficulty here about vision. Firstly, it lacks point of contact the way touch does. Secondly, it seems very difficult to attach sense to the requirement that the seer in order to possess the visible must also be visible. There does not seem to be anything in vision which presupposes being visible in the sense that our having a sense of touch presupposes our being touchable. The only tentative explanation I could offer would be on Hegelian lines, the analogy being that in terms of his pre-supposition of a multiplicity of consciousnesses for the possibility of self-consciousness. Vision and therefore being visible is an essential part of our form of life.

Kant, in the *Critique of Judgment* can be taken as making a very similar point in suggesting that the experience of beauty in nature is hinting at an affinity between the noumenal self of the subject and that of external nature. If taken in the Kantian sense, Merleau-Ponty's point is unexceptionable, but he seems to want to say more than this and as a result insurmountable difficulties arise. He wishes to establish a strictly analogous account for all senses. He says that just as touch is achieved by the movement of the fingers which are spread from within but are also accessible to touch from without, so vision is accompanied by movements of the eyes which are 'felt' and which are accessible to vision, though not directly to our vision.

. . . , we know that, since vision is a palpation with the look [I prefer to translate this as 'feeling with the eyes'], it must also be inscribed in the order of being that it discloses to us; he who looks must not himself be foreign to the world that he looks at.[7]

Thus the seer in order to possess the visible must be possessed by it, be *of* it.

As already mentioned, I find it difficult to make sense of the requirement that the seer, in order to possess the visible, must also be visible. I cannot see how this could be in any way analog-ous to the point that our having a sense of touch presupposes our being touchable—in touching we possess the touchable and are also touched by it. The presupposition is valid in this case because touch, unlike vision, is a contact sense. Merleau-Ponty presents this requirement of reversibility as some kind of neces-sary truth which applies to all the senses. He also extends this to hearing although in the case of hearing the analogy breaks down

completely. Firstly, it would seem that a being must be audible
if it is to possess the sense of hearing. He holds that reversibility
defines the flesh in all its fields. The 'flesh' which Merleau-Ponty
constantly refers to is that which is visible, the outer coatings of
things visible directly to the senses. In the case of individuals, the
flesh is the lived body which is open to the world and permeated
by it. The reversibility involves a constant intertwining between
the lived body which reaches out to that which exists in the world
and responds to it and the things in the world offer themselves
from without. Secondly, he deals here not so much with hearing
but with our sonorous being. Among our many movements are
movements of the throat and mouth which form the cry and the
voice. These movements end in sounds which I hear; I hear my
own internal vibrations. He writes: 'Like crystal, like metal and
many other substances, I am a sonorous being, but I hear my
own vibration from within: as Malraux said, I hear myself with
my throat.'[8]

Thus there is a reflexivity and reversibility of the sonorous
system analogous with that of sight and touch. The analogy seems
very strained because for it to have been strict, hearing would
have to be accompanied by movements in the ear; in a sense this
is so but these movements have to be accessible to hearing and it
is at this point that the analogy breaks down. I have included this
discussion for the sake of completeness; it is of no direct concern
to my topic.

Merleau-Ponty concludes this part by reverting to the unexceptionable point of our adaptation to the world. He says that the
sensitive in general is reversible, that we are all sentient-sensible:

We say therefore that our body is a being of two leaves, from one side
a thing among things and otherwise what sees them and touches them;
we say, because it is evident, that it unites these two properties within
itself, and its double belongingness to the order of the 'object' and to
the order of the 'subject' reveals to us quite unexpected relations
between the two orders.[9]

Our having a being of this kind (this again, I take to be very
close to Kant's discussion of 'our sensibilities') is necessary if we
are to be capable of perception. Merleau-Ponty qualifies the
'leaves' analogy metaphor by saying that the body is not so much
made up of two leaves or two layers because:

C

. . . fundamentally it is neither thing seen only nor seer only, it is Visibility sometimes wandering and sometimes reassembled. And as such it is not in the world, it does not detain its view of the world as within a private garden; it sees the world itself, the world of everybody.[10]

A part of Merleau-Ponty's concern at this point is to stress the objective existence of things in the world and to exclude any kind of Idealism. Perception is possible only for a being which is of the same being as the things it senses. The individual is, therefore, from the beginning palpably *in* the world and a part of it and, what is as important, in an affinity with it. The individual who participates is not to be identified with consciousness; he is his lived body which is open to the world and permeated by it. We can distinguish between the lived body and the world in thought but there is a constant intertwining of the one with the other. The lived body reaches out to that which exists in the world and responds to things which are offered from without. Both body and world exist enmeshed, thoroughly adapted to each other, each permeating the other, in an infinite relation of reciprocity. The relation of reciprocity, however, unlike that of participation, raises the sort of difficulties already mentioned in that whereas we can accept a necessary relation of reciprocity where touch is concerned, such a relation cannot be shown to hold analogously for all senses.

One could object that Merleau-Ponty is in no position to presuppose and stress objectivity or to exclude Idealism in that he has not shown how objective knowledge is possible. This is a very large issue which I do not wish to get involved in here, particularly since it has no direct bearing on my concerns at this stage. One could, in fairness, also argue in defence of Merleau-Ponty that we must judge what he has to say in the context and tradition within which it is said. He is not involved in showing how we come to have concepts; he wants to show what is involved in perception at a stage where we already operate with or apply concepts, where we see things as the things they are. He is directly concerned with what might be termed the process or experience of perception.

Perception for Merleau-Ponty is a sort of complex exegesis, which is dependent as much on the object as on the person perceiving it in the sense that the relationship existing between them (body and world) is such that the spectator talks of himself in it (the object, the world), as much as of it in him.

Here we come to the crux of this account of perception, perception in the full-blown sense that is, in that the relationship which is set up and what is involved in it is akin to what is involved in understanding a situation. The power in the object to provide the perceiver with certain experiences is a power to permeate that experience and invoke others connected with it; it is not simply a question of noting any given feature or features of an object by observation. What experiences the object evokes is to a large extent dependent on the particular experiences of the perceiver although, and this *is* important, Merleau-Ponty (unlike Kant who also hints at similar affinities) rejects any sort of idealism quite explicitly. He insists in fact that in perception we are open to the things themselves, open to them by intertwining, through what might perhaps be termed a creative process in which both the perceiver and object cooperate, hence what I called a complex exegesis is taking place. In reflection we try to objectify the process and can to some extent talk about it in an objectively acceptable way. I say 'to some extent' because this will vary with different situations. Merleau-Ponty also says that since the seer is caught up in what he sees, what he sees is still himself, and that therefore there is a fundamental narcissism in all vision. He holds further that for the same reason the vision which the seer exercises, he also undergoes from the things. This could, perhaps, be interpreted in two ways.

He may mean something akin to many painters who maintain that they feel themselves looked at by paintings and that their activity is in this sense also a passivity. If this is the case, then Merleau-Ponty may mean that the phenomenon is an indication of how much we contribute to the appearance of things we see. He does say that in its coupling with the flesh of the world, the body contributes more than it receives while the visible things inscribe their particular characteristics on our flesh.

On the other hand, if we take into account what he says at the beginning of the chapter (that any red which we see emerges, in a sense, from more general redness and the particular red emerges from a background of reds), then the reciprocity between subject and object is to a large extent dependent on the particular background, particular in the sense that it is particular to a given person. I mean by this that the background is equivalent to the complex conceptual web which a given person employs in perceiving a given object but this is backed up by *his* knowledge of red things. What the red things which he knows are is dependent on his experience of red things.

In addition to the necessity of objectively experiencing a particular thing, this account also stresses the individual's past subjective experiences. Thus Merleau-Ponty's examples of the red of the terrains of Aix and Madagascar which serve as a background to the red dress are a background for him because he knows these particular reds by having had experience of them. Someone else's background may be quite different. Much of this reciprocity goes on on a preconscious level but nevertheless it is part of the very complex background necessary to perceiving something which, on this account, involves more than subsuming a given object under a concept, of identifying it as a such and such. It also involves as it were understanding a given situation which is set up between the subject and the object. The subject throws its style over the things but it has to be a style which they do not reject, one which, because of the subject's kinship with them, is somehow adapted to them. The subject's work of interpretation has to be basically objective.

A word of caution is, perhaps, necessary. When Merleau-Ponty speaks of visible things inscribing their character on our flesh, I take him to mean primarily that, e.g., sounds vibrate in our body, we follow movements with our eyes and so on. But he also seems to imply far more, he seems to want to say that all the visible is flesh as our flesh is. If this is the case, then there must be something which corresponds to the visible. He speaks of external horizons of things knowable to everyone and their internal horizons: 'that darkness stuffed with visibility of which their surface is the limit. Likewise the body is not only its visible surface but darkness stuffed with organs'. It is extremely difficult to make sense of this in all cases of perception. The intertwining of the perceiver with the perceived entails the intertwining on both levels, i.e., the exterior and the interior horizons, the interpretation of both being also very largely dependent on the particular situation towards which both object and subject contribute. One may well ask what the interior horizons are where every object is concerned. Or, in other words, considering the intertwining at stake here it would be difficult to answer the question: 'An intertwining of us and what?' I for one could only answer this in terms of the second interpretation offered above, in that the dark interior horizons are in a way far more dependent on personal approaches than the exterior ones. The former depend more on what one might term selective objectivity. I mean by this that the perceiver applies objective criteria from a variety of such criteria, selecting the ones particularly relevant to his personal experiences. This is rather obscure but Merleau-Ponty seems to hesitate about going into the notion of interior horizons more fully and I think this is because he himself is aware of the difficulties involved.

2.2(b) Perception as Situation Understanding

I wish at this point to extract from the above exegesis what I take to be relevant to my concern. I shall limit myself to a discussion of perception of objects which, although based on Merleau-Ponty's full-blown theory to some extent, will, I hope, avoid the difficulties arising from it. That part of his theory where he speaks of our never perceiving any particular in isolation but always against a background is valid (because of the sort of considerations discussed on pp. 47-48). The intertwining can be equated with the reciprocity, in the sense of participation, between subject and object which is dependent on the particular background against which a particular person perceives.

In perceiving a red thing, the background against which it is perceived is equivalent to the complex conceptual web which is employed by any given person and backed up by *his* knowledge and experience of red things. Perceiving anything involves more than subsuming any given object under a concept; it also involves understanding a given situation which is contributed to by both the object and the subject. This point brings me back to my discussion of content of understanding in Chapter 1. There I argued that an object qualifies as a candidate for understanding on our part (as opposed to knowledge in the sense of acquaintance) only in cases which have specifiable propositional content. What is being understood are certain specific situations surrounding certain particular objects. I went on to say that any situation which someone is trying to understand, or claims to understand, implies that person's participation in it, not merely in the sense that particular aspects of the situation impose themselves on the person but also that the person contributes to the interpretation of particular aspects of the situation.

In the present discussion the account I gave in Chapter 1 undergoes a shift. We are now concerned with complexities of background against which *any* particular is perceived. This background is supplied reciprocally by the object and the subject. Merleau-Ponty's account of perception of objects reinforces my point about the importance of personal elements which enter into understanding. The elements which we contribute to and extract from the object of perception are brought to bear on the interior as well as the exterior horizons of any particular perceived. Merleau-Ponty's account, in so far as I am using it here, provides an explication of personal elements which enter into the perception of any particular in that, although we perceive objects existing objectively in the world, the background against which we perceive them is to a large extent personal (in the sense already discussed). But I cannot extend Merleau-Ponty's theory to show that *all* perception is tantamount to situation understanding (as I use this term). This is due to two main reasons. Firstly, as already indicated, it is well nigh impossible to speak in terms of interior horizons where every object is concerned; one cannot 'supply' interior horizons for every object of perception. Secondly, Merleau-Ponty himself says that we are often not aware explicitly of the relevant things against which we perceive; they remain in the background and cannot be consciously or explicitly identified.

I must, therefore, offer a qualification. In cases of perception where nothing of the background can be specified in propositional form, we have to say that the perception cannot qualify as situation understanding. This is because such cases preclude the fulfilment of my condition of what is to count as a situation surrounding an object: an object qualifies as an object of understanding only where there is a particular situation surrounding the particular object which can be specified in propositional form. In the cases under discussion we cannot state what our participation and the understanding of interior horizons consists in. Thus where the background against which we perceive is not even partly accessible to our consciousness it follows that it cannot be specified in propositional form. For this reason we cannot use the term 'situation' for every case of perception. Yet some complexity in regard to any given particular is guaranteed in so far as we never perceive a naked chunk of being in utter isolation but always against a background and surroundings. The background is provided by our experience of things of the kind that the object of perception is. Thus the stress is on personal elements against the background of which we perceive. We are not passive perceivers—our contribution is characterised by Merleau-Ponty as participation. The elements which we contribute are brought to bear on the perception of any particular perceived. But since that background cannot always, i.e., in every case, be expressed in propositional form, we must reserve the term 'situation' for those cases of perception which fulfil the condition of statable propositional content.

2.3 The Relation between the Perceiver and the Perceived

I now want to turn to situations in the full-blown sense in order to bring out as clearly as possible what is involved in the notion of participation, reciprocity and interior horizons.

As I said above, Merleau-Ponty himself seems to hesitate about going into the notion of interior horizons because he is aware of the difficulties involved in applying this notion to every case of perception and has, in fact, said very little about interior horizons up to this point. I find it very significant that he uses Proust's example from *Swann's Way* (part 2) to throw light on the very difficult connection between the visible and the invisible which is both manifest and concealed. I find it significant because the example involves aesthetic understanding of a sonata. The understanding is based very much on the relationship set up between Swann and the music and through it with the composer. This example can much more easily be seen as a setting up of a situation (in the full-blown sense) and how Swann brings a particular kind of understanding to bear on it because of the kind of person he is. This belongs very much to his world but can nevertheless be objectified. Merleau-Ponty describes the idea involved here as the most difficult point—the relationship or connection between the visible and the invisible: 'We touch here the most difficult point, that is, the bond between the flesh and the idea, between the visible and the interior armature which it manifests and which it conceals.'[11] He says that no one has gone further than Proust in describing an idea that is not the contrary of the sensible but rather its lining and its depth. He refers to a passage from Proust's *Du Côté de Chez Swann*.[12]

The relevant background can be briefly outlined: Swann, in love with Odette, is consumed with jealousy. Attending a concert where a sonata by Vinteuil is being played, he thinks in a most uncomplimentary way about the other members of the audience. He feels contempt for them because they seem unable or incapable of understanding or taking any but a derisory interest in his love. They make it appear to him as if it were a solely subjective state existing exclusively for him, with no external reality to confirm it, almost as if it were a delusion. The sound of the instruments makes him want to cry for being in a place, an exile, where Odette would never come. Suddenly it is as if she had entered. What happened was that the violin had risen to a series of high notes on which it rested as though expecting something. This is a point in the sonata where a certain little phrase is to be introduced. Swann knows the sonata; its structure, form, melodic and harmonic lines, the development of particular themes—in other words, he understands the external horizons of the work, he understands the statable in a way in which it is open to any competent musician to understand.

As with the example of Jean Valjean stealing a loaf of bread, provided the person concerned has the necessary concepts, the factual description of both situations can be stated comparatively simply in that in the one case it is a straightforward description of what took place, and in the other an analysis of a work. But at this point Swann goes beyond this understanding because of a sequence of experiences he undergoes which enables him to understand the sonata (and the little phrase in particular) in a way never before open to him. Just before the little phrase is to be played a host of memories of the days when Odette had loved him, some of which he had hitherto forgotten, come flooding into his mind. But this time instead of abstract expressions like 'the time when I was loved', or 'the time when I was happy' which he was used to repeating to himself, he now remembers things which had fixed the peculiar volatile flavour of his happiness—the heading on the notepaper of a letter she sent him, a cold drive home after seeing her, things she said. He had changed the vague ideas of loving for memories of things that were full of love.

When the little phrase was played, Swann felt protected by a cloak of sound and saw the phrase as a friend who knew and understood his relationship with Odette. For the first time he discovered an element of suffering in the phrase, 'a charming resignation which was almost merry', which he had always previously regarded as expressing a frigid, contracted sweetness. Swann feels pity and tenderness towards the composer who, he now recognises for the first time, must have suffered greatly. 'From the depths of what well of sorrow could he have drawn that god-like strength, that unlimited power of creation?'[13]

The little phrase in no way belittles nor trivialises his love; on the contrary it had captured and rendered visible the essence of an intimate sorrow. It would only appear trivial to anyone who had not experienced these emotions, yet it would still communicate its meaning in some manner. Swann understands the phrase and thinks of it as an idea which is veiled in its sensuous body. On first hearing the phrase he tried to analyse what it was in the music that gave him the impression of a 'frigid, contracted sweetness' and he discovered that it was the closeness of the intervals between the five notes and the constant repetition of two of them. But even at that stage he knew that his analysis was inadequate as it left out something mysterious in the phrase. Now he suddenly becomes aware of an important aspect of a musician's life—he has access to far more than the limits of a seven note stave; he also has access to immeasurable depths of the inner life. Music is not just a voyage of formal discovery for a great composer is able to awaken emotions corresponding to a theme and give us access thereby to the richness and variety which is 'the hidden life'.

Merleau-Ponty agrees with Proust that literature, music, the passions, the sciences and also the experiences of the visible world are the exploration of an invisible and the disclosure of a universe of ideas. But he goes on to say that, unlike the ideas of science, these ideas cannot be detached from the sensible appearances. They are without 'equivalents'. They cannot be given to us or received by us as ideas except in objective experience. They owe their existence, their authority, fascination and power to the fact that they are in transparency 'behind' the sensible and thus interdependent. They are not directly accessible as they are behind the veil of sense; when we try to pinpoint them, they slip our grasp. We are, however, left with an explication which, although it does not give us the idea itself, yields a manageable derivative. In Swann's case it is his ascription of the 'withdrawn and chilly tenderness' to the five notes which compose the little phrase and to the constant repetition of two of them. Here is the phrase's sense or essence. But in putting it thus, Swann somehow lets slip from his grasp the little phrase itself and its idea and is left only with bare values which he substituted for the mysterious entity which he had perceived. The musical idea is only present 'behind' the sounds, as it were, although the sensible texture of the sounds presents to us something that is absent from all flesh; yet it is there, distinct from every other idea, unequal to any in value or in significance. Similarly, concentrations of light present ideas 'without equivalents'; so may, I think, phrases of poetry, sensible and emotional experiences and so on. They are 'able' to present to us what is absent from the sensible, ideas which we cannot possess as we can a positive thought, but which rather possess us.

The performer is no longer producing or reproducing the sonata: he feels himself, and the others feel him to be at the service of the sonata; the sonata sings through him or cries out so suddenly that he must 'dash on his bow' to follow it.[14]

In the previous chapter I spoke of people who seem to have a special ability to understand others. I mentioned the possibility of such persons possessing certain extra concepts which not everyone has and I denied the possibility of settling this question. I am now tempted to think that these special concepts may be of the same kind as those enabling Swann to understand the little phrase in the way he does. They are called to the fore as it were in a particular context, they come into use in a special way according to any given relationship set up in a given situation. It is very important to stress that the situation in which Swann finds himself and the insight he gets which enables him to understand the phrase in a new way is not based on any association of ideas or feelings.

This example could well be contrasted with the well known

'petites Madeleines' episode[15] which is a case of pure association, a recollection of subjective childhood experiences:

> . . . in that moment all the flowers in our garden . . . and the water-lilies . . . and the good folk of the village . . . and the whole of Combray and of its surroundings, taking their proper shapes and growing solid, sprang into being, town and gardens alike, from my cup of tea.[16]

The Madeleines bring about recollections and memories which return with the taste; whereas the understanding which Swann achieves during the concert is a new understanding. There is a new dimension in the little phrase which is utterly lacking in the 'petites Madeleines' incident. The point of the example is to bring out precisely those elements which enable Swann to understand in a new way. At the beginning of the concert he indulges in recollections of the days when Odette loved him, memories come flooding into his mind. But at the moment in which the little phrase is introduced a change takes place—instead of recollecting episodes and vague ideas of loving he now thinks of things which were full of love, he dwells on what love is really like, not specifically his love of Odette but love qua an emotion. Swann would now remember the phrase as a conception of love. It would exist always, sometimes latent in his mind, but there to be brought into use, to be coaxed forth when appropriate. These domains of ideas are the invisible of the world, they are of the world, they sustain it and render it visible. They are the being of this being just as sentience is the being of our own sensible being. Thus the surface of the visible is doubled up, as it were, over its whole extension with an invisible lining. At the level of perception, where in our flesh the visible thing exhibits a visibility, extension and thought come with being together, the one behind the other. Merleau-Ponty writes:

> And what we have to understand is that there is no dialectical reversal from one of these views to the other; we do not have to reassemble them into a synthesis: they are two aspects of the reversibility which is the ultimate truth.[17]

'Pure' ideality streams forth along the articulations of the aesthesiological body, along the contours of the sensible things. I think this throws some light on Merleau-Ponty's notion of the flesh of the world. He seems to want to extend an account of aesthetic perception to perception in general.

Now, it seems to me that whereas his ideas work in a most interesting way when applied to art, especially to music and poetry, to understanding a given situation, Merleau-Ponty gives these ideas an extension with the aim of establishing the existence of a prototype of ideality in *everything* that is sensed. I have argued, in effect, that this cannot be done in the required sense for all cases of sense-perception. Nevertheless, perception in the full-blown sense (involving a complex degree of understanding) demands whatever is involved in understanding a situation and thus the concept of 'situation' is crucial to such cases of perception and understanding. This needs explanation. To return to Merleau-Ponty's account of the perception of a musical idea— some philosophers (e.g., Croce) offer a rather empathic account of emotional qualities in art; others, particularly Bouwsma, maintain that emotional qualities are qualities of Gestalt characters of the work: 'The sadness is in the music as redness is in the apple'.[18] Many others hold that the work evokes or arouses appropriate emotions in us. For Merleau-Ponty the emotional quality of a work is a well-nigh untranslatable signification, or sense of the musical phrase. But when Swann concentrated on the 'little phrase' in order to discover its meaning which he described as 'withdrawn and chilly tenderness', by trying to do this he has silenced the resonance of the idea, a resonance which had not yet been fully actualised. At the moment of his suffering the little phrase with its untranslatable idea had delivered to him the essence of love. Thus the audible, with its invisible lining, obtained access to 'the great, impenetrable and discouraging night' of Swann's mind. For Proust, it is one of the functions of art to make our inner life yield up what lies hidden in its darkness, and so to give us reassurance that our depth is not to be regarded as 'valueless and waste and void' which it so often seems to us to be, although the latter is, perhaps, a more natural or normal state.

Merleau-Ponty, by using the example from Proust, succeeds in illuminating, in a most interesting way, our understanding of how the sensible is a sort of causeway joining exterior and interior horizons. Proust, in describing how the little phrase was related to the immediately preceding part of the sonata, which announced it, described what falls within the exterior horizon. The phrase's resonance, on the other hand, which evoked the vivid idea of love falls within the interior horizon. This part of Merleau-Ponty's work opens up very interesting possibilities for our understanding of the experience of emotional qualities in art. These qualities are not simply of one kind only. What is important is that we can appropriate such varied qualities in a number of ways, receive as it were the emotional content of art.

One might argue that giving vent to one's emotions during a performance is being guilty of a dereliction of one's perceptual duty, of one's aesthetic appreciation of the work. If anything of this kind occurs during the hearing of a musical work, it represents a diversion of attention from the work, a sort of vagrancy. Merleau-Ponty and Proust, however, suggest that it is precisely by provoking the listener to use his understanding based on his own experiences that art can evoke a sensitive awareness; that one way of experiencing any such quality can lead to another way of experiencing another, closely related but nevertheless different quality. This resonance which evokes ideas can amount to an illumination and a freeing of the inner life. Proust suggests that for a person who is sufficiently mature emotionally, Vinteuil's sonata has the power to deliver to him the essence of love. This, it seems to me, is an aesthetic power which demands a special response such as Swann's, although each person would respond in a manner appropriate to him, and this power qualifies us as aesthetically educated hearers. We do not simply allow our subjective emotions to flood over us because this indeed would make us lose contact with the work; the work provokes appropriate understanding in us. This is an objective power though dependent on our particular personal experiences and thus influencing our particular understanding and awareness, regulating what sort of understanding we are capable of.

R. K. Elliott, in his paper 'The Critic and the Lover of Art' writes:

... the extent of our freedom to change our responses through patience and favour has not been generally recognised. This, together with the great variety of modes in which a work may be experienced precludes the establishment of a strongly objective form of critical discourse unless extremely severe and quite unjustifiable restrictions are placed on what is to count as aesthetic response. . . . There could be a large measure of agreement about what constitutes an aesthetic judgment rather than a judgment of some other kind, and a large measure of agreement in aesthetic judgments, without there being any universal aesthetic norm.[19]

To impose a priori very strict limits on what is to count as aesthetic understanding of a work seems too high a price to pay for the possibility of objectivity in such judgments. The importance of objectivity lies in being able to communicate intelligibly one's response, one's understanding of what is going on and, perhaps, thereby to get someone else to understand something they may have missed. But this does not demand complete agreement in judgments as the agreement or disagreement involved is of a different kind from that of which Wittgenstein speaks (in the *Philosophical Investigations* 242) but is nevertheless dependent on it. This provides the possibility of aesthetic agreement or disagreement in judgments, it forms their basis. I think this is what Merleau-Ponty means when he writes:

Why not admit—what Proust knew very well and said in another place—that language as well as music can sustain a sense by virtue of its own arrangement, catch a meaning in its own mesh, that it does so without exception each time it is conquering, active, creative language, each time something is, in the strong sense, said? Why not admit that, just as the musical notation is a *facsimile* made after the event, an abstract portrait of the musical entity, language as a system of explicit relations between signs and signified, sounds and meaning, is a result and a product of the operative language in which sense and sound are in the same relationship as the 'little phrase' and the five notes found in it afterwards? This does not mean that musical notation and grammar and linguistics and the 'ideas of the intelligence'—which are acquired, available, honorary ideas—are useless, or that, as Leibniz said, the donkey that goes straight to the fodder knows as much about the properties of the straight line as we do; it means that the system of objective relations, the acquired ideas, are themselves caught up in something like a second life and perception, which make the mathematician go straight to entities no one has yet seen, make the *operative* language and algorithm make use of a second visibility, and make ideas be the other side of language and calculus.[20]

Perception for Merleau-Ponty involves much more than applying the relevant concepts to something seen, that is by identifying
it as a such and such. Perception always involves a relation between
perceiver and perceived. It always involves, in addition, a more
or less complex understanding of what is 'going on'. But this
understanding, however complicated, is closely tied to and
governed by the object of understanding. Understanding, however, involves the notion of points of view. I have several times
referred to 'the sort of person the perceiver is'. This now requires
explanation. I quoted Spinoza as saying that the particular way
in which we form our concepts is not only accidental (through
sense perception) but is also affected by our interests, desires and
purposes. But our interests, desires and purposes stem, I think,
from what is available to us, what forms a basis for them—our
experiences. Our experiences involve what we have come to know
personally, through personal contact and what we have succeeded
in extracting from this.

At a certain stage the involvement between the perceiver's life
and the perceived becomes so interdependent as to be inseparable. In understanding a situation it is not just a matter of reporting our feelings, facts or even various reactions to a set of circumstances which are immediately objective. In addition we are influenced by what our experiences prompt us to extract and that
is, and has to be, relevant to our understanding of what is going
on. Which aspects our experience enables us to extract is closely
related to our particular interests; our interests will govern our
dispositionally choosing certain aspects as more relevant than
others. The given aspect (or aspects) which our experience enables
us to extract has to be relevant to the object of understanding not
only for reasons of objectifying to some extent what we have come
to understand but also because this understanding is based on a
relationship set up between the perceiver and the object of understanding.

If this relationship is broken, what follows cannot be an understanding of what is going on but a flight of fancy or, as in the case
of listening to a given composition, a giving in to purely subjective
indulgences of one's emotions and so on. In such cases the object
of understanding becomes a means to a subjective end and thus
loses connection, the vital 'causeway' necessary to our understanding. One may ask here: What criteria do we use, how do we

judge when the relationship in question no longer holds, when or at what stage does it break down? The only answer I can offer is that there is no general answer to the question. There must, however, be a possibility of agreement with others about what it is one claims to have understood. When we try to objectify our understanding of a given situation according to the particular aspects we find relevant, it has not only to be meaningful to others but the relationship must be *seen* to hold, at least to some extent. The difficulty is that this cannot be demanded for all cases. The point is that in attempting explanations of understanding of this kind the procedure has to be dialectical; we cannot demand direct proof or anything like it in this context.

Also, the demand that criteria for such understanding be stated a priori is misguided; an a priori account would apply in general whereas we are concerned with particular cases. We have ways of judging whether particular cases of understanding are appropriate by using standards which arise from the nature of the particular case. We use criteria arising from the particular case and these enable us to judge whether what the perceiver is claiming to have understood can indeed be related to the object of understanding. This difficulty, however, is perhaps a necessary and useful one, as it allows us, as in the Swann example, suddenly to change our perception, to understand differently, to notice an aspect we have missed or misunderstood before.

Proust speaks of Vinteuil as the composer who was able to discover secret laws that govern an unknown force driving towards the one possible, right goal. The themes which entered into the composition of the phrase are like premises which come to an inevitable conclusion in the syllogism:

The suppression of human speech, so far from letting fancy reign there uncontrolled (as one might have thought), had eliminated it altogether. Never was spoken language of such inflexible necessity, never had it known questions so pertinent, such obvious replies.[21]

Both Proust and Merleau-Ponty imply a strong analogy between music and language. I do not wish to base my point on such an analogy as there are great difficulties inherent in the view that music is the 'language' of emotions, etc. All I need for my purposes is that music has the power to convey emotions and that its course may have an inevitability about what we have to hear in order to understand it. The composer has to discover the right, inevitable way leading to the one possible, right goal.

A composition provides a necessary framework of understanding, one that cannot be analysed into any logical elements but nevertheless definite enough to demand our appropriate involvement and responses, as opposed to flights of fancy or purely subjective indulgences. The intertwining at stake here is not a one way relation in which the music calls forth our experiences which we then proceed to dwell on; it coaxes us to use our background understanding and bring it to bear on what the music tries to tell us, to deliver to us. In some way we extract from our own experience a great deal which illuminates our understanding of the work. This understanding is of necessity personal, dependent on what we are able to extract but it is in an important way rule-governed and therefore, as I term it, selectively objective rather than subjective in the sense of losing contact with a given situation. Merleau-Ponty makes a very similar point, I think, when he writes:

And, in a sense, to understand a phrase is nothing else than to fully welcome it in its sonorous being, or, as we put it so well, *to hear what it says* (*l'entendre*). The meaning is not on the phrase like the butter on the bread, like a second layer of 'psychic reality' spread over the sound: it is the totality of what is said, the integral of all the differentiations of the verbal chain; it is given with the words for those who have ears to hear. And conversely the whole landscape is overrun with words as with an invasion, it is henceforth but a variant of speech before our eyes, and to speak of its 'style' is in our view to form a metaphor. In a sense the whole of philosophy, as Husserl says, consists in restoring a power to signify, a birth of meaning, or a wild meaning, an expression of experience by experience, which in particular clarifies the special domain of language.[22]

I have offered an exegesis of Merleau-Ponty's chapter 'L'entrelace —Le Chiasme' in order to place what I consider relevant in its proper setting. My main concern, however, was with that part of his account of perception where he stresses the importance of the relation between the perceiver and perceived and it is on the complexities of that relation that I have concentrated throughout. Accordingly, I have tried to enlarge on these issues.

The Swann example throws light on the notion of interior horizons in terms of participation—perception is not passive; our contribution, our efforts to understand the complexities of a situation which is presented are characterised by Merleau-Ponty as participation. In all cases of understanding it is my conceptual background backed by my personal experiences which will determine which factors in a given situation I will find relevant and which I am incapable of understanding. The appropriateness of the understanding can and must be judged in objective terms in that, as I have tried to argue, understanding is internally related to the notion of reacting in a certain appropriate way to what has been understood. The notion of appropriateness presupposes the possibility of objective judgments of inappropriateness.

This point could, perhaps, be put differently by saying that a subject subjectively selects from varied possible appropriate ways of understanding a situation (a musical composition) those aspects which are relevant to him, i.e., arising from what he as subject has been able to extract and contribute. Thus, although the understanding and its relevance is of necessity personal, it is also in an important way rule-governed and, therefore, as I termed it, selectively objective rather than subjective in the sense of losing contact with the situation, in the sense where what the subject takes to be appropriate will be appropriate. It is the situation which dictates what understanding will count as appropriate.

This issue could be made clearer by analogy. In listening to music, it is the music which influences our mood, not our mood which governs the music. We may be in a mood in which we wish to hear some 'cool' music. Accordingly we listen to some Bach and find that we have made the wrong choice. Bach is not 'cool'; his music has proved inappropriate to this particular mood. We may then try some other composer. The point is that our mood did not influence the character of Bach's music. If this should occur then we have in an important way lost contact with the Bach composition and our response and understanding are no longer appropriate. The relation between the music and the listener has broken down. The notion of inappropriateness is necessary for the notion of appropriateness to get any grip.

In a complex case like that of understanding a situation, one which involves many varied aspects, which may be qualitatively different (moral, personal, historical, sociological, scientific, emotional, etc.), *one* appropriate understanding cannot be pre-supposed. Our understanding will depend to a very large extent on our particular interests and our capacities as to which aspects of the situation we are able to understand. I have tried to argue that situations qualify particularly as objects of understanding and have stressed the importance of subjective elements which every person brings to bear on such understanding. It seems to me that the notion of 'situation' can be used to describe most kinds of understanding which take place. Perception of anything particular can never take place in utter isolation—rather we pick out the given particular perceived from a background and sur-roundings which provide a situation around particulars perceived. But it isn't always the case that we perceive the background *as* a background, in which case it would be wrong to say that we perceive the object as a situation, i.e., in giving an account of *the perception* of the object it would be wrong to attribute the term 'situation' to such a case. We can only legitimately attribute the term 'situation' to cases of understanding which satisfy the con-dition of statable propositional content. In addition, the reciprocity between subject and object gets a strong hold in situations in the full-blown sense as was illustrated by the 'Swann' example.

In Chapter 1 I drew a distinction between what is involved in knowing, say, a car and understanding it. The understanding under discussion involved the understanding of some content with regard to a particular object. The point I was trying to make was that an object qualifies as a candidate for understanding (as opposed to merely knowing) only in cases where a particular content which a particular object involves can be specified in propositional form. Understanding, e.g., cars, involves a degree of complexity which merely knowing what cars are does not. Thus in cases where we make the contrast between knowing x and understanding x, we stress the difference between knowing some-thing simpliciter and understanding the situation (content) with regard to that given something.

In this chapter I have tried to point out that a situation which one is trying to understand implies a given person's involvement in it, not merely to the extent that the situation imposes itself on the person concerned but, as importantly, what the given person contributes to it in his attempts to understand. In trying to understand a situation we extract and contribute to a greater or lesser extent and the mode of involvement is based largely on subjective elements.

I have given an example which concentrated on those aspects which we extract from our experience, which illuminate our understanding. These aspects represent our personal contribution to understanding. Thus, in arguing that situations qualify particularly as objects of understanding, I have stressed the importance of subjective elements which every person brings to such understanding; *how* a person contributes and *what* he extracts. The degree and kind of involvement regulates the degree and kind of understanding. It is for this reason that I have spoken of perception and understanding as a creative process within the context of reciprocity which is set up between perceiver and perceived, which is tantamount to a situation having been set up.

Given the above arguments, the understanding of persons has to be investigated in terms of kinds of situations which are set up in various cases. The notion of reciprocity which brings out personal elements is crucial in the particular context of person understanding and must form a significant part of any such investigation. The reciprocity we spoke of as 'interaction' between subject and object now becomes interaction quite unequivocally. The notion of reciprocity takes on great importance in reference to persons and will therefore need extended discussion in following chapters.

In addition, persons are paradigmatically candidates for understanding because the existence of complex situations is presupposed in their case. This is because, as I have argued in the previous chapter, we have prior knowledge, stemming from our understanding of the kind of thing persons are in general, that each and every person is a complex object and the understanding of such an object must necessarily involve the understanding of many facets. Thus both my conditions necessary for something to count as an object of understanding, i.e., the existence of some content surrounding the object and the expressibility of that content in propositional form, are fulfilled in the strongest possible sense where person understanding is concerned.

It is for these reasons that understanding of the self and of others qualifies as situation understanding in the primary sense and I shall now turn to examining what is involved in the understanding of such primary or paradigmatic situations.

Notes

1 P. Geach, *Mental Acts*, Routledge and Kegan Paul, 1957, Sec. 4, p. 7.
2 Merleau-Ponty, *Le Visible et l'invisible*, ed. Gallimard, Paris, 1964. All references are to the English translation by A. Lingis, edited by C. Lefort, published by Northwestern University Press, 1968.
3 Merleau-Ponty, 'L'Oeil et l'esprit' appeared in the inaugural issue of *Art de France*, Vol. 1, No. 1 (Jan. 1961), reprinted in *Les Temps Modernes*, No. 184-5.
4 Carleton Dallery (tr.), 'Eye and Mind', in *The Primacy of Perception and Other Essays*, ed. J. Edie, Northwestern University Press, 1964.
5 *Op. cit.* p. 132 (see note 2).
6 *Ibid.* p. 133.
7 *Ibid.* p. 134.
8 *Ibid.* p. 144.
9 *Ibid.* p. 137.
10 *Ibid.* pp. 137-8.
11 *Ibid.* p. 149.
12 M. Proust, *Du Côté de Chez Swann*, Part 2, ed. Gallimard, Paris, 1945, pp. 182-94.
13 M. Proust, *Swann's Way*, trans. C. K. Scott Moncrieff, Vol. II, Pt. 2, Chatto & Windus, 1971, pp. 176-88; p. 181.
14 Merleau-Ponty, *op. cit.*, p. 151.
15 M. Proust, *op. cit.* Vol. I, Pt. 1, pp. 58-62.
16 *Ibid*, p. 62.
17 Merleau-Ponty, *op. cit.*, p. 155.
18 O. K. Bouwsma, 'The Expression Theory of Art', in *Aesthetics and Language*, ed. W. Elton, Basil Blackwell, 1954.
19 R. K. Elliott, 'The Critic and the Lover of Art', in *Linguistic Analysis and Phenomenology*, ed. S. C. Brown and W. Mays, Macmillan, London, 1971.
20 Merleau-Ponty, *op. cit.*, p. 153.
21 M. Proust, *op. cit.*, Vol II, Pt. 2, p. 186.
22 Merleau-Ponty, *op. cit.*, p. 155.

3 Persons in Relationships

HAVING the concept 'person', having, that is, an understanding of what this involves, is, perhaps, a necessary condition for understanding particular persons; but whereas we can attempt to give a general account of the concept 'person', no such general account, in terms of sufficient conditions, is possible for individual cases of understanding, as what may be sufficient in some cases need not be so in others. Much will depend on how deep the understanding has to be in a particular case. Having said this, however, it seems to me that some necessary conditions can be specified.

Where the concept 'person' becomes important is at the level of direct experience of persons, because, to put it in Merleau-Ponty's terms, our understanding of a particular person can never take place in isolation. Merleau-Ponty's notion of individuality which he applies to material objects and qualities such as colour, as we perceive them, stems from a particular person's perception of them in that I perceive a particular red always against a background of reds within my personal experience. We can never perceive any object or quality in isolation. In the same way, we can never view a person in isolation from the background of other persons and our understanding of them within our personal experience; this is necessary, a part of what counts as having the concept.

3.1 The Concept of the 'Personal'

When attempting to analyse a concept like that of the 'personal', the question which almost immediately springs to mind is whether there is only one or more concepts involved here?

It is very tempting to suppose that since our contact with other persons is different from any contact with objects, therefore every such an encounter is in this sense personal. So it undoubtedly is, but it also seems clear that putting it this way is saying something rather minimal—it is drawing our attention to a difference of category; I am confronted with a person or I stand in a certain

72

relation to a person and not simply an object. Thus any relations in which one may stand to persons become equated with personal relationships and it is at this point, I think, that confusion arises.

One way in which this confusion can be highlighted is by discussing what is involved in the contrast between the notions of 'personal' and 'impersonal' relationships. That this contrast is a valid one seems obvious but in trying to spell it out certain difficulties become apparent. The very fact that we have and use this contrast is in itself enough, I think, to show that not all 'person' encounters are personal. If we do not accept this then we become confronted with an apparent paradox of a relationship which is both personal and impersonal at the same time. This cannot be right as it stands and therefore the confusion which gives rise to it needs a closer examination.

We could offer an explanation of the apparent paradox by arguing in terms of 'person perception'. One kind of person perception is seeing the given person under different aspects. At this point I am mainly concerned with what I take to be two basic aspects—seeing a person as a person and seeing the person as the particular kind of person he is. Whether I know person x as x or not will affect how I perceive him—as a person in general or as an individual of a particular kind. Our perceiving any person involves, I think, seeing him under one or both of these aspects— either as a person in general or as a person of a particular kind; and the latter will necessarily involve perceiving him under both aspects. This distinction, however, does not seem to me to be very illuminating as it stands without some further discussion of conceptual issues arising from it.

We could, perhaps, ask what conceptual differences are involved in the two different aspects. In the first case, seeing a person as a person amounts to having the concept 'person' in the sense that one knows what sort of thing a person is and is able to identify persons as such on encountering them. This in itself requires the employment of a very complex conceptual web, while in the second case of seeing a person as a particular individual there is required, in addition, the identification of him as that particular person (it minimally involves this). But the notion of the particular individual—seeing z as the particular individual that he is— does, I think, involve on a deeper level having the concept of what it is for someone to be a person of a particular kind. That concept, in itself, quite obviously involves a multiplicity of concepts without the understanding of which we would be quite unable to grasp the complex notion of what it is for someone to be a particular person of this particular kind. For convenience sake, however, I shall refer in this context to 'the concept' of what it is for someone to be a person of that kind. We are concerned here with a particular person in a particular life situation which, in many ways, is exclusively his. Seeing a person under this aspect is seeing him as a particular kind of object of understanding as opposed to seeing him simply as a person which requires only an understanding of what it is to be a person.

It might be helpful, in order to stress this distinction, to speak of the latter as a case of applying a concept which is one of first level and of the former as applying concepts which are employed at the second level (concepts which are employed in understanding what it is for someone to be a person of that particular kind). Here some degree of special understanding is needed in that one has to engage in thinking about the particular situation confronting one in order to arrive at a certain level of understanding of a given person as a person of a particular kind. My distinction between first and second level concepts is one of generic and specific identification respectively. I use the terms 'first level' and 'second level' in order to stress the logical priority—the concept of what it is to be a person of a particular kind is considered as second level because that concept, and its possibility of application, presupposes the first level concept of 'person'.

I now wish to argue that my full understanding of the other is only possible when I stand in relationship to him both as object and as subject. This needs expanding. I think that we can safely rule out seeing a person *purely* as a material object because someone who always did this would be judged as a person who failed to have an adequate conception of what it is to be a person. Thus, for our immediate purposes, seeing a person as an object involves seeing him as an object who has a subjective side. (I shall use 'object' in this sense throughout the chapter except when explicitly specifying otherwise.) Seeing a person as an object involves, broadly speaking, observing behaviour, expressions, deducing motives and intentions from observed actions and such like. Seeing a person as a subject involves seeing him as having feelings, intentions, desires, etc., which come into play in his relationships vis-à-vis another.

The distinction between seeing a person as an object and seeing him as a subject is, at this stage, rather crude in that the opposition, as set out, is very simplistic. It stresses the contrast between seeing a person in terms of externals and seeing him in terms of his subjective side. Strictly speaking the above is not meant as a contradistinction but rather a shorthand way of indicating priorities of concern and interest. Ultimately the distinction turns on the kind of relationship one takes up to another person. I shall return to it in detail.

At this stage it already seems clear that my distinction between first level and second level concepts cannot simply be equated with seeing a person as an object and seeing him as a subject respectively. This is because the understanding at stake in first level concepts is employed in both cases—seeing a person as an object and/or seeing him as a subject. But seeing a person as a person of a particular kind, i.e., applying second level concepts, also involves understanding particular things about the object which has been individuated as a person of a particular kind; the possibility of this kind of individuation depends on an understanding of things about the object—things which apply to the object which is of this particular kind.

We can now return to the original difficulty of the seeming paradox of a relationship which is both personal and impersonal at the same time. The paradox dissolves when attention is drawn to the distinction between first and second level concepts in that the concept of the 'personal' as applied on the first level is tantamount to our engaging in making a category distinction between 'person' and any other object. The term 'personal' is applied to the object of the relation where we stand in person to person relation as opposed to, e.g., person–material object relation. This usage of 'personal' has no implications for any judgments as to whether the relation is also one involving an impersonal relationship. The term 'impersonal' is a further characterisation: it may be an attitude, relationship, outlook, approach and so on and as such it is not the contrary of 'personal' as used above. The term 'impersonal' makes a subqualification within the class or category of 'personal'.

The term 'personal' is ambiguous and the ambiguity arises,

I suggest, from a blurring of important distinctions in usage. The contrast set up above can be presented as follows:

In applying first level concepts, 'personal' characterises any person P which is individuated from any other object. P is here identified under the first level concept 'what it is to be a P'. This is a case of individuation *between* categories.

In applying second level concepts, 'personal' characterises 'a person of this kind' as distinguished from 'a person of that kind' where 'a person of this kind' is identified under the second level concept of specifying kinds of things *within a category*. This involves understanding something of *this* particular kind of person on the strength of which specific individuations are made.

'Impersonal' is the contrary of 'personal' when we begin to employ concepts on the second level, and on this level it would indeed be contradictory to hold that one's relationship to a particular person is both personal and impersonal at the same time. We subqualify particular relationships into personal or impersonal relationships within the category of persons.

What I have said so far does not really clarify the distinction between the notions of 'personal' and 'impersonal'; it is, therefore, to analysing this distinction as well as that between seeing a person as an object and as a subject, that I must now turn. We are, at this stage, concerned with what I called second level concepts which involve some degree of personal understanding. I shall try to examine this in terms of various relationships both personal and impersonal thus, I hope, clarifying the distinction between those relationships.

3.2 The Notion of a Relationship

Given, as I said above, that the terms 'personal relation' or 'personal relationship' are used indiscriminately when applying first level concepts, I shall, for the sake of clarity, use the term 'personal relation' in such cases as distinct from 'personal relationships' which will apply only at the second level.

I suggested that there exists a link between second level concepts and our understanding of a given person. This is because when applying second level concepts within a relationship, whether personal or impersonal, we engaged in an understanding of the given person at some level; here some degree of understanding on an individual level is needed. One has to engage in thinking about the situation confronting one in order to arrive at a certain level of understanding of the given person as the kind of person he is in order to individuate on the second level. If this is so, then any account of personal and impersonal relationships must run parallel with an account of understanding persons. We have to take into account that there are kinds and degrees of understanding; understanding which goes well beyond that which is needed to individuate a person as a person of a particular kind. We are now concerned with the question of what is involved in understanding a person with whom we stand in a personal or impersonal relationship.

It may be useful to return briefly to my previous discussion of what it is to know and understand something. I argued that situations were paradigmatic subject matter of understanding. To take my example of Jean Valjean, I may know exactly what took place—that he stole a loaf of bread, how he stole it and I may also find out further facts such as why he did this—and yet I may lack an understanding of the situation because in an important way I cannot understand the situation without also understanding the kind of person Jean Valjean is. It is in cases of this kind where knowledge gained by observation of external behaviour may lead one completely astray. We are often prone to put hasty interpretations on such external 'evidence' and we do this precisely when the person concerned is unknown to us.

It is in such cases that imagination, normally of great importance in aiding our understanding of others, may lead us badly astray. A quotation from Goethe is rather pertinent:

. . . how easily a superficial idea is taken up by the imagination and how then man persuades himself that he has grasped some truth with his intellect; . . . (if) one notices how complacently he thinks he *understands* something which in reality he only *knows* . . .[1]

My level of understanding of a person's situation is dependent on the particular relationship in which I stand to him. The relationship provides the possibility of an independent check on my imagination such that the person's actions, attitudes, moods and direct responses may draw attention to aspects which have been misunderstood. Being purely an observer precludes any notion of a personal relationship, because relationships, whether personal or impersonal, involve at a minimum level some interchange taking place as opposed to simply a confrontation. This I take to be a crucial difference between personal and impersonal relationships on the one hand, and personal relations on the other.

Being an observer enables me to know that such and such took place, that such and such a man acted in a particular way and so on, but if we go beyond this we become involved in dealing with relationships and situations. My understanding of these cannot be achieved by compiling more and more facts *about* the person concerned except on a fairly superficial level. Facts may tell me much about the attributes of a person, they supply knowledge about the person which obviously involves understanding; but this understanding is on a different level from the kind of understanding which is involved in understanding the person himself in that I have no direct access to the person in the former case, I am forced to deduce possibilities from observed or reported events only without the possibility of the sort of check mentioned.

Factual information, such as may go into a personality profile, may increase our knowledge about a person and may also be an important aid or factor in the understanding of that person but only if another condition is present and that is personal acquaintance with him. This condition is necessary for personal understanding which depends on direct access to the person as opposed to being informed about him. These different factors are decisive for the depth and quality of understanding which is achieved. Since any personality profile, however complex, is simply a complicated synthesis of abstractions, it could never give any personal insight and understanding of that person.

What, I think, emerges is that in order to understand a person at a deeper, personal level, one has to stand in some kind of personal relationship to him thus being in a position to have personal insights, to have direct experience of how his thoughts and feelings find expression in reciprocal relationships. It is only in reciprocal personal relationships that these aspects have a chance of spontaneously and fully manifesting themselves.

The question which now arises is whether any kind of personal acquaintance qualifies as a personal relationship of some kind and, further, what is involved in the notion of personal relationships. It seems fairly obvious that personal acquaintance, although a necessary condition, is not a sufficient condition for personal relationships. We may work with people, live with them or otherwise associate with them for long periods of time without ever coming to any deep understanding of them or particularly wanting to understand them in that way. We see them as role playing individuals and judge them, form our opinions of them, on the basis of the quality of role fulfilment. Our judgments here already involve understanding but this is limited to such aspects as enhance or impair role fulfilment—observing, finding out certain facts, being aware of their states of mind; that they are tired, depressed, or in pain. Curiosity may prompt one to find out reasons for these states and this may involve discussions of personal problems. Help may be offered and yet any true personal element is completely lacking; these actions are seen as a duty which is a part of the given person's role. It is precisely such cases, where the persons concerned are seen exclusively as role playing agents, which fall outside the scope of personal relationships. Yet some sort of person to person confrontation is taking place, and in this sense something personal, which involves a particular level of understanding, is going on.

The above seems an obvious case of an impersonal relationship as well as one where the person concerned is seen as an object only and not really as a subject. One is concerned here with very limited issues. What is more, it seems that the person is seen as an object with very particular, limited functions—those which are deemed pertinent to his particular role fulfilment. Can we then conclude that impersonal relationships are to be equated with seeing a person only as an object?

At this stage, I think, we can already say that, if there is a relation between impersonal relationships and seeing a person only as an object, it is not a symmetrical relation because seeing a person as an object of a particular kind may take place in personal *relations* which rule out impersonal relationships since the former apply at the first level and the latter at the second level. We cannot, however, as yet answer the question raised by the alternative side of the relation, that is whether all impersonal relationships involve seeing a person as an object. Before this can be answered, a closer look is necessary into the distinction between seeing a person as an object and seeing him as a subject.

3.3 Persons as Object and Subject

This brings me to the distinction which Strawson draws in this context.[2] Strawson's main aim is to try to reconcile what he calls optimist and pessimist determinist theses. This topic is not relevant here but in the course of his paper Strawson discusses the distinction I am very much involved with—he speaks of it in terms of an objective attitude in contrast to a personal attitude of involvement and participation. He writes that these are not exclusive of each other but profoundly opposed to each other.

To adopt the objective attitude to another human being is to see him, perhaps, as an object of social policy; as a subject for what, in a wide range of sense, might be called treatment; as something certainly to be taken account, perhaps precautionary account, of; to be managed or handled or cured or trained; perhaps simply to be avoided, ... The objective attitude may be emotionally toned in many ways, but not in all ways: it may include repulsion or fear, it may include pity or even love, though not all kinds of love. But it cannot include the range of reactive feelings and attitudes which belong to involvement or participation with others in inter-personal human relationships; it cannot include resentment, gratitude, forgiveness, anger, or the sort of love which two adults can sometimes be said to feel reciprocally, for each other. If your attitude towards someone is wholly objective, . . . though you may talk to him, even negotiate with him, you cannot reason with him. You can at most pretend to quarrel, or to reason, with him.[3]

Strawson draws this contrast in order to show that in the case of an objective attitude it does not make sense to hold a person, towards whom we hold such an attitude, fully responsible for his actions. Our attitude of resentment and blame is greatly inhibited or modified. Thus, for Strawson, what is involved in an objective attitude is that the person towards whom this attitude is held is in an important way not seen as a person because his freedom as an agent is seriously impaired either morally or rationally. Thus, it seems to me, he uses the notion of 'objective attitude' in a very restricted sense. He argues, rightly so I think, that we can never maintain a wholly objective attitude to any person (who is a free agent) however minimal our contact with them. He goes on from this to speak of involvement and participation which is always present to some degree in inter-personal relationships. 'Involvement' is used here in the minimal sense of contact and possible response which need not involve any real understanding of a person, only an understanding of a given action of his towards us to which we respond accordingly. I take the notion of involvement here to imply something like our commitment to common practices. Strawson speaks of commitment in terms of the fact of our natural human commitment to ordinary inter-personal attitudes: 'This commitment is part of the general framework of human life, not something that can come up for review as particular cases can come up for review within this general framework.'[4] For him, commitment here means simply that by virtue of our form of life we respond to others in certain ways, ways about which, basically, we have no choice because how we respond, in general terms, is an integral part of what it is to be a human being; or, to put it differently, understanding the appropriateness of our responses to others is a part of the concept 'person'.

Strawson does say, however, that the simple opposition of objective attitudes and the various contrasted attitudes 'must seem as grossly crude as it is central.'[5] He goes on to say that parents and others concerned with the bringing up of children cannot hold either kind of attitude in a pure or unqualified form. This is because children, although increasingly capable of holding human and moral attitudes, are not *fully* so capable. The question arises whether all adults are 'fully capable' of holding and sustaining both the human and moral attitudes in every situation in which they may find themselves. The answer must be, I think, that they are not so capable for a variety of reasons: they may be incapable of adequately understanding the situation they find themselves in; they may be rather shy and this will prevent them from reacting in a way in which they would wish to react; or they may simply not be sufficiently interested in others in general and therefore will not respond fully. Nevertheless, several important lines of enquiry arise from Strawson's discussion and I shall pick these out in the course of the next few pages, enlarging on their significance in a different context.

It seems to me that by virtue of our natural human commitment to ordinary inter-personal attitudes it is quite impossible (in cases of interaction) to see persons merely as material objects; or even to make no attempt whatever to go beyond first level concepts without in any way holding some personal attitudes which open the way to personal understanding.

Seeing a person as an object is not, however, to be equated with an objective understanding of that person. Without objective understanding no other kind of personal understanding would be possible. Having the concept 'person' involves more than just seeing the person as an object, it includes seeing him as an object of a special kind; first level concepts already involve the notion of a person such that it is recognised that a person is the kind of thing which possesses both an objective and a subjective side. It is, therefore, tempting to suppose that since we all, as persons, share the same form of life, this gives us a rather special vantage point from which to exercise this special kind of knowledge which is termed as understanding of persons. Thus, one might argue, there is really no special problem: our understanding of persons stems from the form of life which we all share, from shared experiences, shared learning and so on. So it does, and the argument holds if it is directed at stressing the importance of the role objectivity plays, objectivity which stems from shared, because inter-subjective, experiences. This gives us an account of how understanding persons in general is possible, but it is not enough as an account of understanding different particular individuals.

It is often said that we understand well those people with whom we have had close contact in early childhood. The basis for our understanding is our knowledge of their particular circumstances and history as well as the fact that we have followed the same rules, learned and enriched our concepts under their guidance, adopted their moral and other views. This, I think, is too simple an account of personal understanding. It will serve as a truncated account of a child's development through personal relationships with its parents or its mother in particular. But it fails to take into consideration the fact that children brought up in the same environment, sharing the same experiences, having the same things put in their way, still turn out to be different as persons. Although experiences influence our becoming the kind of person we are it is important to note that the same experience may affect people differently.

What has been said so far focuses on how a child acquires understanding in general, a part of which may be his coming to know what it is to have a personal relationship, but it does not follow from any of this that the child has personal understanding of the mother. This kind of example sets up rather particular problems but I do not think that the difficulties stem simply from the child's failure to hold what Strawson terms 'fully developed' moral and human attitudes. The problem, as I see it, still holds when the child reaches the age where he is 'fully capable' of these attitudes; although a parent/child relationship is certainly a personal one, it is also (among other factors such as the personalities involved, their circumstances, the generation gap, family relationships in general, etc.), very much circumscribed and dependent on the roles of the individuals, the roles they have to take up. These are in no way rigid, according to some set rules of appropriateness; they will vary according to particular parents' notions of what is deemed appropriate. It is, I think, to a large extent because of the role playing involved that the personal relationship is limited in the sense that it limits or sets up boundaries to the personal understanding possible.

Whereas roles determine what is an appropriate relation to things, this is not clearly the case with personal relationships. On the one hand, such relationships may go well beyond any roles from which they originally stem and, on the other, certain roles may prevent the relationship from developing, hence the difficulty with parent/child relationships discussed. In such cases the adherence to what is appropriate to those roles becomes an inhibiting factor. If the relationship develops beyond the initial roles then the notion of appropriateness becomes very complex partly because, as I mentioned before, personal relationships rarely remain static and, with their development, what is appropriate also changes and is modified.

In spite of these complexities and their accompanying difficulties, the conceptual link between the notion of appropriateness and the concept of a given thing or person remains not only valid but of utmost importance in connection with the fact that we cannot sustain wholly objective attitudes to persons. One's understanding of what is appropriate to a person qua object of knowledge and understanding is very relevant to one's attitudes towards another in inter-personal relationships. These are in an important way not *just* a matter of understanding what is appropriate (this is a part of first level concepts) but also of understanding that once we stand in a relationship, whether personal or impersonal, the attitudes which are appropriate cannot be purely objective in Strawson's sense, they cannot be such in the strong sense that we have no choice in the matter.

To see another and consider him *purely* as an occupant of a role without at the same time considering his point of view as a human being is, I think, a paradigm case of an impersonal relationship. The question which could be raised here, and this is closely related to the notion of appropriateness and the concept 'person', is whether such an attitude, say, to a colleague, involves a lack of respect for the person concerned and, further, whether any what might be termed impersonal relationships entail lack of respect for persons. Is an impersonal relationship incompatible with seeing the occupant of the role as a person? I think the answer must be a firm 'no' unless the occupant of the role is seen *purely* as a thing to be used for carrying out certain purposes. There is such a wide range of impersonal relationships that they cannot be equated with a failure to see someone as a person. Respect for persons is very closely tied up with the concept 'person' and this includes certain reactions on our part to persons which do not, however, demand anything approaching a personal relationship. We may act out of a moral obligation, humanitarian considerations and such like, all of which would show the required respect for persons and yet be quite impersonal. Respect for persons demands primarily that persons must not be treated as things, used or manipulated to one's own ends; in other words persons, in Kantian terms, must be seen as ends in themselves. But none of this entails entering into personal relationships.

Strawson's distinction between the objective and personal attitudes, although it brings out the most important point that we cannot sustain wholly objective attitudes to persons in interpersonal relationships, is, however, rather limited because the purely objective attitude in his sense is limited to one towards persons who in one important way or another are not seen fully as persons; some of the essential attributes of persons in general are lacking here. For this reason his distinction will not do as an account of what is involved in seeing a person both as an object and as a subject. It is, therefore, necessary to look at this distinction in some other way.

3.4 Personal and Scientific Knowledge

Supposing we say that it is open to any individual to isolate himself from another particular individual or group in the sense that he does not wish for a personal relationship to develop. One can only really know another person, as that person, by entering into a personal relationship with him. What then is it that one is isolating? Without the necessary condition of standing in a relationship, whether personal or impersonal, my knowledge of another is only possible by observation, inference and fact gathering. The former enables personal understanding of others which is the result of reflection upon our personal or impersonal dealings with them, recognising these persons as different from each other in important respects. The latter type of knowledge could be described as scientific knowledge. I prefer this contrast to 'objective knowledge' which is, I think, rather misleading.

Objective knowledge does not necessarily entail viewing people as objects; on the contrary, having the concept 'person' already prevents us from this and in an important way objective knowledge enters very much into personal understanding. Nevertheless, scientific knowledge, although valid, is in an important sense abstract knowledge because it precludes the knower from knowing and understanding a whole range of things pertinent to the person concerned. Many things about a person can only be known through entering into a relationship, whether personal or impersonal, which enables the development of personal attitudes to take place.

Thus, what is important is that once we stand in any kind of relationship with a person, personal attitudes begin to play a lesser or greater part in our understanding of him. In such cases the knowledge and understanding we begin to acquire is no longer to be equated with scientific knowledge as such; it is no longer abstract because it is no longer disconnected from personal attitudes.

I said at the beginning that knowing a certain number of attributes or characteristics of a person does not constitute a real understanding of that person. What then is the range of aspects which one is precluded from knowing and which a given person can intentionally isolate? Each of us is a self in that we exist for ourselves as well as for others, we come to understand ourselves and others through our interaction with others in a common form of life. But each individual has a private life of thoughts, hopes, feelings and emotions which, although largely dependent on others, do not *necessarily* figure explicitly in his objective life and cannot, therefore, be absorbed by or accessible to others. These aspects are profoundly different in kind from overt aspects and it is at this point that, I think, the distinction between a person as object and as subject begins to emerge.

Before going into detail, one point needs to be stressed. I do not wish to imply that the distinction between personal and scientific knowledge is one which is more or less equivalent to knowledge based on subjective and overt factors respectively. On the contrary, I have explicitly argued that both kinds of factors are necessary for personal knowledge and understanding. Conversely, as I hope to show, scientific knowledge of a person may include knowledge of how his feelings, thoughts, etc., find expression. Furthermore, knowing someone as a person is not simply tantamount to knowing his subjective side. Having said this, I am not in any way denying the importance of the fact that persons have a subjective life and that without this there would be nothing personal to know and understand.

Now, the distinction between a person as an object and as a subject hangs on different things that can be said of a person. For instance, overt characteristics, it seems to me, are only one class among others within which what can be said of a person is contained. What can be said about personal data such as a person's date of birth, etc., belongs to the class of facts about him. But there is also a class which covers those aspects which belong to the category commonly referred to as the privacy of the personal life; what can be said of a person here can only in principle be said of any given person. I say 'in principle' because we cannot be certain in any way when the circumstances will obtain which will be conducive to our being in a position to do so in fact. I don't mean to imply that there is no possibility of anything being said in fact. I wish rather to stress the possibility that what can be said of some of the aspects of a given person, belonging to this class, may not be said of the given person in fact, because these aspects may not become explicit in our transactions with him. Yet they may or may not be implicit and thus discoverable in certain particular circumstances within a particular persona relationship which will enable personal understanding on a deep level. The difficulty is not about what can or cannot be said but about circumstances obtaining such that will make saying something possible. I shall enlarge upon what may be involved in this kind of understanding in a separate chapter.

What I am concerned with here is the distinction between different circumstances having to obtain for what can be said of characteristics and facts about a person on the one hand, and what can be said of the subjective life on the other. The distinction rests mainly on conditions which allow the possibility of access to these various aspects.

Acquiring knowledge of overt characteristics and facts about a person could be said to require on the one hand, where the person is not known personally, conditions where information is gathered indirectly or by observation, where something like scientific method is employed, where hypotheses which are postulated can be tested by gathering the information necessary to the confirming or denying of them. This type of information is usually accessible and thus discoverable regardless of the wishes or intentions of the person about whom it is gathered.

On the other hand, in cases where we stand in some kind of direct relationship with the person concerned, access to the various classes listed above is certainly direct, first-hand access and may or may not also be indirect. What is important here is the manner in which our knowledge of characteristics and facts is acquired. If it is acquired without any personal (direct) knowledge of the person concerned and without direct communication then it comes very close to Strawson's notion of an objective attitude in as much as we are precluded from holding any personal attitudes in these cases (cases of scientific knowledge). This is very different from coming by knowledge of characteristics and facts about a person with whom we stand in some kind of direct relationship, because here personal attitudes play a vital part as does the question of what is appropriate.

When one is concerned with the subjective life the issue becomes more complex. Here one can intentionally or otherwise isolate oneself from circumstances which may become conducive to these aspects being made explicit or implied. One is, to a large extent, in control as it were. It is important to stress in this context that the various classes of what can be said of a person are not straightforwardly exclusive of each other in that seeing a person as an object, which involves acquisition of knowledge of a person's characteristics and facts about him, does not preclude one from coming to understand anything at all of his subjective side.

In the case of personal understanding it seems clear that seeing a person both as object and as subject is essential. What can be said about a person's overt characteristics and facts about him is interrelated with what can be said about aspects which the given person finds profoundly important in his subjective life. Without knowing a person's characteristics and certain facts about him, we could not understand him at a deeper level because, it seems to me, knowledge of them forms a basis on which personal relationships can develop.

It can, I think, be seen now why the distinction between personal and scientific knowledge cannot be equated with knowledge based on subjective and overt factors respectively. Personal knowledge and understanding is and has to be based on both factors. Similarly, scientific knowledge based on observation and gathering of information may result in an understanding of both subjective and overt factors. But the *quality* of the understanding *is different*. It is only in reciprocal personal relationships that subjective aspects of a person's life have a chance of spontaneously and fully manifesting themselves. Attitudes, purposes and reciprocal responses are of crucial importance here. But these are lacking in cases of scientific knowledge. The point is *not* that we cannot come to know a person's subjective side in cases of scientific knowledge but rather that the resulting understanding is limited and qualitatively different. We have no experience of the reciprocal development of understanding.

This being the case, it may be objected that, after all, scientific knowledge is precise, because uncluttered by personal attitudes and is thus more likely to be correct and, therefore, constitutes the only valuable kind of knowledge of persons. To argue in this way is, I think, to construe knowledge of persons on the model of knowledge of material objects.

Philosophers who take this latter view also usually hold that emotions, which to a greater or lesser extent play a part in personal relationships, are either apt to lead us into error or they are so idiosyncratic as to be of no relevance and thus have no place in any philosophical theory of knowledge of persons. It is indisputably true, I think, that very often too close an emotional involvement may blind us to certain aspects of, say, the other's character or intentions towards us and we may need to try taking a more detached view. But equally, an absence of any feeling precludes us from the closeness necessary for a deep understanding of the person. Even strong emotions like love, hatred or fear may often sharpen our awareness and focus our attention and apprehension thus leading to an understanding of some important truth about the person concerned which might otherwise have escaped us.

It seems to me that both scientific and personal knowledge allow of error but to prefer the former is to fail to allow for considerations arising from the sort of thing a person is and, I suspect, from a prejudicial preference for scientific explanation in general.

To understand another on a deep level is not just to see him as object and subject but also *to understand* him both as object and as subject. The crux of the matter is how we come by this understanding; the quality of the understanding is dependent on qualitatively different approaches.

It is just as important to our deep understanding of a person to know many of his characteristics as it is to understand those aspects which he can either intentionally or through unconscious intention withdraw or prevent from figuring explicitly in his transactions with various others. In the latter case coming to understand is a question of mutual learning as opposed to just coming to know in isolation from the person concerned. This involves at least shared time or shared activities; not simply, say, sporadic exchanges of confidences but a growth of understanding which develops through responses and an involvement one with the other, an involvement which brings in feelings or emotions and is based on the whole range of interpersonal attitudes which Strawson draws our attention to. A purely objective attitude, in Strawson's sense, to any person we come into direct contact with, have transactions with, is impossible, nor can we speak in this context of scientific knowledge; in these cases the knowledge is direct knowledge of characteristics and facts which leads either to personal or to impersonal understanding.

Hegel's example of the master/slave relation may serve to illustrate most of these distinctions. The relation as described is

objective in Strawson's sense in that the master uses the slave
merely as a tool, a means to an end; consequently he fails to
regard him as a person and instead sees him as an object with
certain capacities to be utilised. This relation, so far, does not
even qualify as a personal relation which already presupposes
seeing the object as a person. The attitude which the master has
to the slave arises out of convenience and needs careful cultivation
in that the master wishes to suppress or deny that at the same
time he probably holds certain opinions about the slave based on
personal characteristics of obedience, humility, cheerfulness or
otherwise, his understanding and efficient carrying out of commands—these belong to the personal in the sense that he cannot
fail to see the slave as a person, a person with whom he stands in
an impersonal relationship. But the master allows or encourages
the non-personal aspects of the relation to dominate thus inhibiting the development of any personal elements. Such an attitude,
though not wholly objective since this would, as Strawson says,
be impossible, involves deliberate self-deception on the master's
part and also raises the important point that it is parasitic and
dependent on personal attitudes. If the master can be said to
have the concept of person then it is incumbent on him to explain
why he treats the man as a tool; it would not be incumbent on
him to offer explanations or justifications as to why he treated
him as a person if this were the case.

It would seem then that one important difference between
scientific and direct or personal understanding is that the last two
require personal contact and, further, that this personal contact
already precludes a purely objective attitude in Strawson's sense.
It does not, however, preclude seeing the person as an object in
my sense nor does it exclude completely any elements which
belong to seeing the person as a subject. The point is that these
may or may not be present; the personal attitudes are there as
the basis for seeing the person as a subject but whether this aspect
is developed in any way or not depends on particular circumstances, particular, that is, to a given case. How these develop is
significant. For instance, to argue that a part of what is involved
in a personal relationship as opposed to an impersonal one is that
the person concerned feels free to unburden and discuss his
problems, is not enough. It seems to me that as a criterion of a
personal relationship this simply will not do. An obvious counter-

example is the relation between a patient and his psychiatrist—here the relationship is deliberately an impersonal one *and* the patient is seen as an 'object for treatment'; this does not preclude the psychiatrist from seeing him also as a subject but by virtue of this special professional relationship there is, and has to be, a strong intention to prevent any development in this direction.

Two people, on meeting, already begin to form opinions about each other, having feelings, however minimal. These are constitutive of embryonic personal relationships. But contact, however close or sustained, is not enough. There is, for instance, the rather popular view that people who have shared a common life for long periods come to understand each other to such an extent that they know what the other is thinking or going to do even though there may not be any behavioural signs present.

To hold this view without qualification is to fail to take into account a very important distinction between kinds and levels of understanding. We may know what the other is thinking or going to do because through a long association we have learned about his habits, reactions and such like. On this level real personal understanding of that person's subjective life need not be involved. We come to know a vast number of characteristics and facts which can be attributed to that person and understand him in this sense as an object—a person of a very particular kind; we may also recognise him as a subject and yet fail to understand whole areas of what is of utmost importance to that person. We may know and understand much and yet not have the deep understanding which can only develop within a personal relationship; because this relationship does not predominate even though all sorts of personal attitudes are present.

I said above that a psychiatrist's relationship with his patient is an obvious case of an impersonal relationship and deliberately so. This statement may invite strong objections; these objections have to be met.

M. Schleifer, for example, tries to argue against just the kind of point I have made.[6] As a large part of his article is also an attack on Strawson's position, it seems very pertinent to our purposes particularly since what he has to say tends to underline, very tellingly, the sort of confusions which are so prevalent in the area of various interpersonal relationships.

3.4(a) Strawson's Objective Attitude versus Interpersonal Relationships

Three main issues are raised in Schleifer's article:

1. The claim that we cannot evaluate the behaviour of persons, except superficially, without the use of psychological explanations.
2. The claim that Strawson's description of the objective attitude in terms of seeing a person as an object for treatment is wrong.
3. The claim that a therapist or clinician, far from being detached must, in order to be good at his job, hold the full range of reactive attitudes, including involvement, which Strawson is said to preclude.

I shall take the three points in turn. It seems to me that this whole discussion is invaluable for clarifying the issues with which we have been concerned so far.

1. Schleifer starts his paper as follows:

Is there any legitimacy in the use of psychological explanations ('Ps-explanations' for short) in our ordinary interpersonal relations? In what way can Ps-explanations rationally affect our evaluations of what people do as well as what they say? P. F. Strawson's British Academy Lecture, 'Freedom and Resentment', has as a main theme the denial of the legitimacy of using Ps-explanations in our normal relations with people. I shall attempt to clarify the use of psychological explanations by considering two special kinds of relationships: that between an adult and a child, and that between a therapist and his client. I shall then argue that Strawson is wrong to depict these relationships as relevantly different from so-called 'normal' ones and consequently that Ps-explanations may affect our evaluations of what any person does or says.

He then goes on to give a definition of Ps-explanations as any explanations which go beyond the immediately obtainable verbal answer by invoking general knowledge of behaviour. Knowledge of behaviour is meant to include knowledge of what men do and say as well as what psychologists speak of in terms of movements and glandular secretions. He concludes this section by saying:

It is perhaps mistaken to attempt any more precise definition for an admittedly vague term. It will perhaps suffice to note that smiles, tears and blushes, as well as speech and physical acts, should all be understood as 'behaviour' in the relevant sense.[7]

So far, there is nothing in Strawson's article which could be taken as a criticism or objection to the above. What Schleifer's definition of Ps-explanation amounts to, philosophically speaking, is that in order to understand what one particular person does we need to understand what people in general do. This also fits in with my distinction between first and second level concepts of person in that we individuate persons from other objects by the application of the first level concept 'what it is to be a person' (which includes understanding what sort of things people do) as opposed to second level concepts the application of which characterises 'a person of this particular kind' as distinguished from 'a person of that kind'.

In fact, as far as I can see, Strawson has nothing, directly, to say about Ps-explanations as such and in as much as he discusses, in general terms, what people do, how they react in situations, etc., he could be said to offer Ps-explanations in the sense of Schleifer's definition.

Why then does Schleifer think that Strawson 'has as a main theme the denial of the legitimacy of using Ps-explanations in our normal relations with people'? It seems to me that Schleifer equates Ps-explanations with objectivity, i.e., with objective, and therefore also rational, explanations. He then links objectivity with Strawson's notion of the objective attitude thereby falling into the trap of thinking that Strawson rules out Ps-explanations in ordinary interpersonal relationships.

It is quite obvious that Schleifer does not really come to grips with Strawson's notion of the objective attitude, a point which will be made much clearer in the next section. But, as I argued earlier, seeing a person as an object (taking up the objective attitude) is not to be equated with an objective understanding of that person. The latter applies in all cases of person understanding; the former covers very exceptional cases only, cases which demand some explanation as to why an objective attitude has been taken up.

But at this point Schleifer's argument about Ps-explanation undergoes a significant shift. He writes:

Ps-explanations—like medical ones—are tied to attempts at changing the behaviour in a direction which is considered better. They are more adequate, provided they give us this ability to handle, treat and change the behaviour in desired directions.[8]

Two questions immediately arise: Ps-explanations are more adequate than what? Change of behaviour is to be affected as desired by whom? He gives a kind of answer:

We now have an answer to the question: why are Ps-explanations more adequate? They better serve the needs of the situation—either the need to help a person change as in therapy, or the need to make an evaluation concerning questions of culpability and punishability.[9]

Unfortunately, our questions remain unanswered. Schleifer says that the ends of Ps-explanations (change of behaviour) are clearest in the special cases of therapy and modifying child behaviour but the same ends are part of normal personal relationships although this is less obvious.

It is . . . obvious that a therapist is involved in changing the behaviour of a person; this is also made explicit at the beginning of therapy. Might it not be that Ps-explanations have the same legitimate role in our normal interpersonal relations—namely as part of the process of evaluating and changing the behaviour of the other and oneself?[10]

According to Schleifer, we modify our tendency to blame others, in our interpersonal relations, by attempting to eradicate the blameworthy behaviour rather than reinforcing it with hostile reactions. He gives an example of a person habitually boasting about his achievements. By applying a Ps-explanation we see the behaviour as the result of pressures towards acceptance and affection. If we did not attempt Ps-explanations and instead used a superficial characterisation we would react with hostility thus reinforcing the behaviour we wish to eliminate. Schleifer goes on:

However, in view of the Ps-explanation of this behaviour, it becomes *irrational* to react with hostility and blame. In the final analysis it is rational to employ Ps-explanations to alter our ascriptions of culpability because we will thereby help achieve the behaviour and relationships that we want.[11]

Could not the Ps-explanation which Schleifer offers be seen as a superficial rationalisation? Perhaps the man just *is* boastful. We would need to know much more about the person concerned before we could judge with any confidence what is, in fact, the case. This raises a very serious issue about Ps-explanations with reference to non-ascription of blame and the whole question of responsibility. There is strong and widespread opposition to this tendency in psychology. Regretfully I cannot discuss this issue further as its scope would require a separate book. Schleifer could be taken, somewhat ironically, to advocate the sort of procedure which Storr so vividly warns us against. He wants to extend the use of generalised Ps-explanations while Storr advocates rightly, as I have argued, that we must withdraw projections and pre-judices of the past; to dispel the smoke-screen of what we imagine a person is like and replace it with the reality of what he, in parti-cular, is actually like.

What emerges so far is that the issue between Schleifer and Strawson is not about Ps-explanations as such, since Strawson has nothing to say on the subject, but rather about what Ps-explana-tions are *used for* and how they are used. This brings us to the second claim.

2. Schleifer writes, quoting Strawson:

When using Ps-explanations in our interpersonal relations, one is clearly adopting an attitude which Strawson would describe as objec-tive: 'To adopt the objective attitude to another human being is to see him, perhaps, as an objective of social policy; as a subject, for what, in a wide range of sense, might be called treatment. . . . Personal, reactive attitudes . . . tend to give place, and it is judged by the civilised should give place, to objective attitudes, just in so far as the agent is seen as excluded from ordinary adult human relationships by deep-rooted psychological abnormality—or simply by being a child. But it cannot be a consequence of any thesis which is not itself con-tradictory that abnormality is the universal condition.'[12]

It is fairly clear from the above comment on Strawson, that Schleifer, as I have suggested, misunderstands Strawson's position regarding the objective attitude. Nothing that Strawson says implies that every therapist must adopt the objective attitude in every case of treatment. What he does say is that we can only take up an objective attitude to a person if, *and only if*, he is in some way incapable of taking part in ordinary adult relationships by virtue of some deep-rooted psychological abnormality. But, and this is an all-important 'but', if using Ps-explanations logically entails the changing of behaviour, handling, manipulating, affecting changes 'in the desired direction', etc., then it becomes more plausible to say that Strawson would consider their use as a necessary part of the objective attitude mainly because persons are entities who must not be used, manipulated or handled under normal circumstances. Schleifer goes on:

Since I have argued that Ps-explanations typically used with children and in therapy can legitimately be extended, it would seem that my thesis does entail that normal relations are universally abnormal, and is contradictory. This argument . . . is based on . . . questionable assumptions. First there is the implicit acceptance of one overall normality–abnormality distinction. However, this dichotomy cannot be assumed in any simple form; . . . . Another possible assumption underlying this argument is that an explanation implies 'abnormality'. This view of explanation is surely mistaken. There is nothing in the logic of a Ps-explanation which demands that the explicandum be in any sense abnormal.[13]

I agree that there is nothing in the logic of Ps-explanations, in the sense defined, which demands that the explicandum be in any sense abnormal, nor does Strawson imply this. Neither does he accept, implicitly or explicitly, one overall normality–abnormality distinction. Schleifer takes Strawson's description of the objective attitude as seeing a person as an object for treatment quite literally without taking account of Strawson's qualifications. I mean here that Schleifer takes Strawson as saying that any person who stands in need of treatment is a candidate for the objective attitude. But it is obvious that just any departure from the norm is not enough to inspire an objective attitude. A patient suffering from some disease is treated by his doctor but that, in itself, has no implications for what kind of attitude is going to be taken up. Strawson stresses repeatedly that:

. . . , our adoption of the objective attitude is a consequence of our viewing the agent as *incapacitated* in some or all respects *for ordinary interpersonal relationships*. He is thus incapacitated, perhaps, by the fact that his picture of reality is pure fantasy, that he does not, in a sense, live in the real world at all; or by the fact that his behaviour is, in part, an unrealistic acting out of unconscious purposes; or by the fact that he is an idiot, or a moral idiot.[14] (My italics.)

Strawson is not concerned with an overall normality–abnormality distinction, because the sort of case he is concerned with is one about the marked abnormality of which there can be no doubt. These are extreme cases which are startling, vivid exceptions and indubitably recognisable departures from the norm however vaguely one takes this term. Nothing that Strawson has to say is supposed to imply that any patient is to be seen as a candidate for the objective attitude merely by virtue of being a patient, of needing treatment.

3. Schleifer writes that the claim made by Strawson that a therapist must suspend his ordinary personal and moral attitudes is quite false. Indeed it is false but in the sense that Strawson does not claim this. What Strawson says is that an objective attitude *is only possible* where the person is seen as an object for treatment in the special cases described above, *not* that an objective attitude *must be* adopted in every case of treatment.

Schleifer then goes on to say that the psychotherapeutic relationship is by very definition an interpersonal relationship. As such it cannot involve the cancelling of human emotions and reactions. He allows that it is 'a very special kind of relationship in which there is an explicit attempt to understand, explain and modify behaviour. Yet nothing follows from this about lack of involvement'. He adds that, on the contrary, it is a fundamental principle that we may become more involved in a relationship by making the effort at understanding. I am sure that no-one would dispute the truth of this principle per se.

Schleifer quotes several clinical authorities, among them C. Rogers, who argues that any therapist who would 'suspend his emotions' just cannot be a good therapist. It is not only false that a therapist can deny feelings or 'suspend his personal reactions'— it is absurd.

Now, if a therapist is capable of the full range of reactive attitudes, including involvement, in a given case then, ex hypothesi, he is not adopting the objective attitude and nothing more need be said. That case is not one where it is *impossible* to be involved in an interpersonal relationship (the crucial criterion of the objective attitude). Strawson's strongest point is that whatever attitude we adopt, we have no choice in the matter. The last word in this context must, I think, be Strawson's:

What *is* wrong is to forget that these practices, and their reception, the reactions to them, really *are* expressions of our . . . attitudes. . . . Our practices do not merely exploit our natures, they express them. Indeed the very understanding of the kind of efficacy these expressions of our attitudes have turns on our remembering this.[15]

The objective attitude is profoundly opposed to personal attitudes which occur in interpersonal relationships.

This brings me to my original remark that a psychiatrist's relationship with his patient is an obvious case of an impersonal relationship.

We have now delimited clearly, I hope, the scope of the objective attitude and we are at this stage concerned with the range of interpersonal relationships. I have already indicated that this range contains personal as well as impersonal relationships. Schleifer says that the psychotherapeutic relationship is by its definition interpersonal. So it is, and I am not denying this, but it still leaves open the question whether it is a personal or an impersonal relationship. To say that such a relation is inter-personal is to generically identify the relation, an identification which applies at the first level discussed. When we come to identify such a relation as personal or impersonal, we employ second level concepts of specific identification.

I have identified the therapist/patient relationship as an obvious case of an impersonal relationship and I need to defend this position in view of what Schleifer has to say. He admits that there are specific rules about the limits of involvement, rules which are codified with specific punishment for regression. The implication is obvious. These rules are professional rules, they establish and prescribe the roles of therapist and patient. If these roles were transcended, the relationship would change and we would then need to re-assess it. The therapist *primarily* offers a service for which he receives payment. The service offered, as Schleifer himself states repeatedly, is that Ps-explanations are involved as a first step in an attempt to change or 'treat' the behaviour which gave rise to the necessity for Ps-explanations. He extends this argument to claim that Ps-explanations have the same role in our usual interpersonal relationships, '. . . namely as a part of the process of evaluating and changing the behaviour of the other and oneself'.

Now, the overriding argument in support of my original identification is, I think, that persons in personal relationships do not necessarily, if at all, wish, *primarily*, to change the behaviour of the other and/or of the self. This is not what such relationships are about, this is not their main or even secondary aim while it is the sole aim of the therapist. Further, the very use of the term 'therapist' inescapably underlines the 'patient' evaluation and treatment. It follows logically that if a patient goes to see a therapist he goes in order to receive some kind of treatment. The word 'patient' (although Schleifer, significantly, replaces it by 'client') presupposes some kind of disturbance. It is this logical fact which entails a role relationship with the sort of limitations discussed and with a specific end in view; these factors are constitutive of impersonal relationships. No such limitations or specific ends apply in personal relationships.

The distinction I am concerned with could, perhaps, be highlighted by an analogy from aesthetics. R. K. Elliott in his article 'The Critic and the Lover of Art' (referred to in Chapter 2) writes:

It is possible to distinguish two common types of approach to art. One I attribute to a person I shall call 'the critic' since critics often adopt it, the other to a person whom I shall call 'the lover of art'. Nowadays critics assert not that the work must impose its authority on a totally disinterested spectator but that it must be received sympathetically 'on its own terms'. This is a fair description of the lover's attitude. The difference between them emerges in their respective practice. Ultimately it involves differences in the kind of being attributed to the work and in the part which Art plays in the life of the individual, ... The work becomes a part of his life not in the trivial sense that it has occupied his time but in the sense that it has engaged him in his depth and, it seems, has revealed its own depth to him.

Both the critic and the lover of art receive the work of art sympathetically, 'on its own terms'. In the same way the therapist and the person who stands in a *personal* relationship to another 'receive' the other sympathetically, 'on his/her own terms'. The very telling difference between them emerges in their respective practices. Ultimately, and crucially, everything depends on the kind of *being* attributed to the other person and on the part that person plays in one's life. In the case of the therapist, the practice consists of attempts to change behaviour in some way, there is a definite end to strive for. By very strong contrast, persons in personal relationships do not set up any kind of general, invariable end. The relationship becomes a part of their life, not in the trivial sense of occupying the time of the persons concerned but in the sense that they are engaged deeply and unreservedly, that they are in a position to better understand themselves and the other in a *mutual*, ongoing relationship.

3.5 Personal and Impersonal Relationships

It may be argued that, for instance, a teacher's attitude to his students is an impersonal one (in the sense of being detached) and therefore what I have said about personal contact (confrontation), and the personal attitudes which accompany such confrontations, does not hold. This objection rests, it seems to me, on certain tacit assumptions which give rise to a confusion of important distinctions. An example which highlights this confusion is given by R. S. Peters.[16] A student attending a seminar, during a boring exchange between two other students, takes out the *Good Food Guide* and begins to study it whereupon the lecturer sends him a note with the name of a restaurant on it. This is taken by Peters as an example of '. . . a personal relationship, though a minimal one, even though nothing further develops in the way of private disclosures'.

Now, it seems to me that personal relationships, however minimal, cannot be simply isolated episodes. This way of looking at it fails to take account of the most important distinction between personal reactions and attitudes on the one hand and personal relationships on the other. It would be most misleading to construe any personal gesture as a personal relationship. I have also argued that any personal confrontation already precludes a purely objective attitude and thus impersonal relationships, such as the teacher/student example in the objection above, do not and cannot exclude personal attitudes; they are not to be taken as in any way incompatible.

Personal attitudes are simply a natural response which is a part of the general framework of human life, they are an integral part of what it is to be human. Our intentions are not necessarily involved in this whereas in personal relationships they are of paramount importance. In addition, I think, Peters' example also shows that what the lecturer responded to was the *Good Food Guide* and x's interest in it, any x who happened to study it might have elicited the same response. What I mean is that the important point of the example is not the student as that individual person; any other student who happened to be doing the same thing would, most probably, have done just as well. This, surely, stresses the impersonal aspect.

Having said this, I want to stress the distinction in a rather different way before going on to an attempt at giving a positive account of the notion of a personal relationship. Let us take a fairly common example of certain women who, at their first meeting are, within minutes, exchanging confidences about their children, husbands, illnesses, etc. At subsequent meetings they carry on the interrupted confidences and thus a relationship develops, one which is rich with all sorts of personal attitudes and personal responses. Can this be seen as a personal relationship? As it stands, my example is rather underdescribed but it will, I think, serve my purpose. Eric Berne calls such a relationship a game. A word of qualification is needed here as it seems to me that Berne takes an over pessimistic view of interpersonal relationships; I do not think that people play games to the extent implied in the book but the distinctions he makes will, perhaps, help to explicate those I have been concerned with. He writes:

Pastimes and games are substitutes for the real living of real intimacy. Because of this they may be regarded as preliminary engagements rather than as unions, which is why they are characterised as poignant forms of play. Intimacy begins when individual (usually instinctual) programming becomes more intense, and both social patterning and ulterior restrictions and motives begin to give way. It is the only completely satisfying answer to stimulus-hunger, recognition-hunger and structure-hunger. Its prototype is the act of loving impregnation.[17]

Now, psychological jargon apart, I understand the distinction drawn to centre on what may be termed social contact and personal contact. Games fall under the description of social contact and Berne defines them as follows:

A game is an ongoing series of complementary ulterior transactions progressing to a well-defined, predictable outcome. . . . Games are clearly differentiated from procedures, rituals, and pastimes by two chief characteristics: (1) their ulterior quality and (2) the payoff. . . . Every game, . . . is basically dishonest, ...[18]

By strong contrast, a necessary condition for something to count as a personal relationship is, negatively speaking, an absence of any ulterior (which I take here to mean self-gratifying) element and thus any calculating procedures. On the positive side personal relationships involve a degree of sustained (as opposed to sporadic) outgoingness and spontaneity both of approach and response. Games involve role playing in a very strong sense where important aspects of a person's private side (as opposed to his being an occupant of a role) do not enter into consideration. The person concerned is not seen, is not accessible in terms of an individual, a human being with certain hopes, feelings, aspirations.

It might be tempting to conclude from this that what is needed in order that the personal relationship may develop is that the person concerned be seen by me simply as an individual which in turn involves isolating the individual from the role he plays or the position he holds in respect of, say, his job. This, I think, would be a mistake. The job a person does is very much a part of him as a person and an understanding of him involves in large measure an understanding of his attitude to his job, what it means to him, how much a part of him it is and so on. The point at issue is that he must not be seen purely in this role nor must he be seen in isolation from it. Although his role is an important part of him as a person, this need not preclude the development of a personal relationship which rises beyond it. This is not to deny, however, that in many cases the roles of the individuals concerned are such that they do preclude any possibility of a personal relationship developing. Nevertheless these issues do, I think, support and spell out why I stress the importance of having to see a person both as an object and as a subject within a personal relationship which in turn opens the possibility of personal understanding at the deepest level to take place.

Thus, I hope, it can now be seen that seeing a person as an object and seeing him as a subject on the one hand, and impersonal and personal relationships on the other, cannot be equated. Seeing a person both as object and subject is a necessary condition for personal understanding, whereas personal and impersonal relationships are exclusive of each other, even if there is no clear-cut boundary between them because within impersonal relationships personal attitudes, which are present, can develop and thus at a certain stage there is a significant overlap.

Having said all this there are relationships which appear to pose difficulties for my account. For instance, what of the case of pen friends of long standing who have come to an understanding of each other at a very deep level, where beyond a doubt, a very personal relationship has developed and yet what I take as an essential condition for such understanding is lacking; they have never met. It is difficult to see what can be said here with any degree of confidence beyond observing that these cases are parasitic on paradigmatic cases of such relationships. The persons concerned are seen by each other both as object and subject and in an important sense a confrontation is taking place, they are responding to each other, are involved with each other, yet never directly. But it follows that there are significant areas in their separate lives to which the other has no access. What is here being understood is a person built up in the imagination of the other, developing out of what has been learned in the correspondence. The issue, it seems to me, hangs on what would count as mistaken understanding in this context. There is no independent check, as it were, which is available in paradigmatic cases where a person's actions, attitudes, moods and direct responses may draw attention to aspects which have been misunderstood. In this sense access to areas of understanding and of what can be said of a person is denied in fact as well as in principle. It is for this reason that I do not think such cases can serve as serious objections to my account.

Notes

1 Goethe, 'A Contribution to Optics', in *Pure Colour*, by Maria Schindler, New Culture Publications, London, 1946, p. 10.
2 P. F. Strawson, 'Freedom and Resentment', in *Studies in the Philosophy of Thought and Action*, ed. P. F. Strawson, Oxford Paperbacks, 1968.

3 *Ibid.* p. 79.
4 *Ibid.* p. 84.
5 *Ibid.* p. 90.
6 M. Schleifer, 'Psychological Explanations and Interpersonal Relations', in *Philosophy and Personal Relations*, ed. A. Montefiore, Routledge & Kegan Paul, 1973, p. 170.
7 *Ibid.* p. 171.
8 *Ibid.* p. 174.
9 *Ibid.* p. 174.
10 *Ibid.* pp. 174-5.
11 *Ibid.* p. 176
12 *Ibid.* pp. 181-2.
13 *Ibid.* p. 182.
14 P. F. Strawson, *op. cit.* p. 83.
15 *Ibid.* p. 96.
16 R. S. Peters, 'Personal Understanding and Personal Relationships', in *Understanding Other Persons*, ed. by Theodore Mischel, Basil Blackwell, Oxford, 1974, p. 54.
17 E. Berne, *Games People Play—The Psychology of Human Relationships*, Penguin Books, 1971, p. 17.
18 *Ibid.* p. 44.

4 Understanding as a Creative Process

I ARGUED in the previous chapter that the knowledge and understanding of a given person which results from a scientific approach does not, and cannot, constitute a deep understanding of that person. Knowledge obtained in this way is qualitatively different from knowledge and understanding which develops within a personal relationship. It is only in reciprocal personal relationships that subjective aspects of a person's life have a chance of spontaneously and fully manifesting themselves. Attitudes and reciprocal responses are of crucial importance—these are lacking in cases of scientific knowledge. The point at issue here is *not* that we cannot come to know anything of a person's subjective side in cases of scientific knowledge but rather that the resulting understanding is limited and qualitatively different. The distinction between scientific knowledge and personal knowledge rests on the fact that different circumstances have to obtain so that qualitatively different kinds of knowledge and understanding result.

At this point an attempt has to be made at some explication of the conditions and circumstances conducive to personal understanding on a deep level.

We are concerned here with circumstances which enable us to see and have experience of a person both as subject and object within a personal relationship which involves, as I have argued, a degree of sustained (as opposed to sporadic) outgoingness and spontaneity both of approach and response. This necessitates a mutual feeling of confidence on the basis of which reciprocity can take place. The notion of reciprocity is, I think, vital for any personal relationship to exist. This way of looking at it is, of course, as old as Aristotle who lays stress on this very point in his account of friendship and speaks also of the importance of mutual trust and feelings: '. . . ; but how could one call them friends when they do not know their mutual feelings?'[1] But, more importantly, personal understanding involves, minimally, some communication and this in itself is reciprocal. By communication I do not mean merely the use of language but wish to include the rich variety of non-linguistic communication such as expressions, looks, gestures and actions which enter into our experience and cannot, often, be verbalised. My understanding of the other is, to a large extent, not simply dependent on my feelings, attitudes and actions towards him but also on his expression of his feelings and his attitudes and actions towards me. These are an important part of the reciprocity involved in any personal relationship, reciprocity which enables a mutual growth of understanding to take place. If such reciprocity is withdrawn it entails a refusal to act in a spontaneous manner and is replaced either by role or game playing and this, in turn, amounts to my hiding myself from the other thus preventing the other from really knowing or understanding me. It is particularly in such circumstances that scientific knowledge, which involves knowledge acquired through observation, can be most misleading since this kind of knowledge is based on the assumption that a man's observed behaviour is the sole or main context in which understanding takes place.

This view fails to take account of the fact that persons, paradigmatically, have the choice between acting naturally or of being misleading by refusing to act spontaneously. I do not wish to imply that we cannot come to some understanding of such a person but I think such a person inhibits the development of a personal relationship which is essential to a deep understanding of him. To put it differently—it is not the case that in order for me to understand someone at all that person must to a large extent wish it and act accordingly. It is rather that in order for a personal relationship to develop and be sustained the persons concerned must allow and wish for it to be developed, by being themselves; and it is this essentially reciprocal personal relationship that is necessary for deep personal understanding.

4.1 The Concept of Sympathy

Before I go on to develop the above, I think it is necessary to mention two rather widespread approaches to personal understanding which I take to be rather misleading but which carry with them important implications. The concept of reciprocity is often associated with that of sympathy existing between two people. But 'sympathy' as normally used is mainly associated with the notion of responding in some way to the *suffering* of another. The response may be that of pity, compassion and the like. This usage does not reflect the full meaning of the term and it is, therefore, inadequate for expressing the complexities inherent in the concept, for making explicit what is involved in it. I rather suspect that the common usage of the word is closely tied to feelings of pity and compassion because it is easier and more usual to sympathise with someone in their misfortunes than it is in their joys and successes. This may be so not merely because such a response comes naturally; such a response may also stem from moral considerations such as seeing it as one's duty to help someone in need, be it physical or emotional, whereas there is no such implication of duty present in connection with people's joys and successes.

I may feel deep pity for a person I do not even know but of whose misfortunes I have heard; in such a case there is no question of my understanding the person concerned except in terms of vicarious responses. In the context of personal relationships this kind of sympathy is, therefore, inadequate; it becomes merely a personal attitude. I am referring here to the distinction made in the previous chapter between personal relationships and personal attitudes which are always present to some extent in any kind of personal contact whether the contact takes place within personal relations or within personal or impersonal relationships. Personal acquaintance fosters personal attitudes; we have no choice in the matter as we can never maintain a wholly objective attitude (in Strawson's sense) to any person, however minimal our contact with him. A personal attitude is, at its most neutral level, merely a certain appropriate response to any given person by virtue of his being a person (where first level concepts only need be employed). That is why, I think, the example given, which involves sympathetic, vicarious responses, is an instance of merely a personal attitude where any real understanding of the unknown person is precluded.

It may be objected that I have dismissed the concept of sympathy, and the work it does in personal understanding, too lightly, that it carries a wider meaning than the one I allowed for. I must, therefore, briefly examine the wider meaning. In physics, for instance, the word is used in reference to sounds produced by responsive vibrations induced in one body by transmission of vibrations by another. Other uses cover notions of agreement, harmony, accordance with one's feelings or inclinations, affinity, agreement in disposition, nature, etc., by virtue of which things are similarly affected; a tendency of one towards another and so on. Thus, I think, the strongest implication the concept 'sympathy' carries is that of fellow feeling, but in a much wider sense than simply that of pity or compassion.

The wider account of sympathy seems to suggest that an essential element in sympathy is that of affinity; the attraction of like to like, and it is very tempting to suppose that this kind of affinity must lie at the root of personal understanding. But then it is not clear whether personal understanding could ever exist between two people very different from each other. H. T. Martineau for instance writes: 'It was impossible that there could be much sympathy between two men so unlike.'[2] Now, if sympathy in the wider sense (with its necessary elements of harmony, accordance, affinity, etc.), is to be taken as a necessary condition of personal understanding, then it follows that two people very different from each other could not achieve such understanding because no sympathy could exist between them.

I think that the concept of sympathy is rather misleading in the context of personal understanding and personal relationships because it fails to account for cases where deep understanding is possible and quite compatible within personal relationships based on antipathy, marked differences and even hate, for instance, in the case of Iago and Othello.

Thus, it seems to me, we have, prima facie, two accounts of sympathy as a necessary condition of personal understanding but, paradoxically, it emerges that the narrow account is also too wide (it allows cases where understanding of a person with whom one sympathises is not involved and thus 'sympathy' here is neutral as a condition of understanding), and the wide account is also too narrow (it excludes cases where deep understanding is possible and quite compatible within personal relationships based on antipathy, marked differences and even hate; thus sympathy is not a necessary condition of understanding). In both accounts the concepts merely overlap.

What I have said so far does not really answer the question whether two people very different from each other could achieve personal understanding. I don't think this question, as it stands, can be answered in general terms; much would depend on the respects in which they differed—whether culturally, in character, interests, beliefs and so on. Nevertheless, the concept of affinity carries with it strong implications of something shared, some harmony. The only way I can think of answering the question is in terms of the balance obtaining between affinity and difference in any given relationship. This is rather an empty answer because I think the problem here is centred on the concept of affinity quite independently from the concept of sympathy and until some light is thrown on what specifically is meant by it we will get no further.

Before considering the concept of affinity and indicating the direction in which I see its importance to lie, I wish, briefly, to mention the second approach which has become particularly fashionable since the 1920s. This is the concept of empathy which raises particular problems.

4.2 The Concept of Empathy

Historically the concept of empathy stems from the Greek use of 'Empatheia' and was originally used mainly in an aesthetic context. One definition is: 'The power of projecting one's personality into, and so fully understanding, the object of contemplation'. As far as understanding works of art is concerned, I find this a rather attractive definition because it seems to stress that aspect of aesthetic appreciation which, above all, requires projection on the part of the spectator, an 'opening out' to receive what the work has to deliver to us. An important kind of reciprocity is thus set up between the work of art and the spectator. But if we try to adapt the definition to cases in which the object of contemplation is a person then, I think, certain difficulties follow regarding the work which empathy is supposed to do. The modified definition would read: 'The power of entering into another's personality and imaginatively experiencing his experiences'. The analysis both of the Greek word and the German version supports this adaptation since the Greek 'em-pathos' literally translates to 'in-feeling', and the German 'Einfühlung' to 'Ein' (in) + 'Fühlung' (feeling).

Empathy, then, involves the notion of putting oneself in the other's place. What precisely is meant by this? There are, I think, at least two ways in which this could be done:

1. Putting myself in his place could be taken as equivalent to trying to understand how *I* would feel in his place or situation.

2. Putting myself in his place could also be taken as trying to understand how he feels in the situation he finds himself in. The first alternative need not involve any real understanding of the person concerned; at most it need involve only a certain understanding of the situation itself and what *my* responses or feelings towards it would be like—this allows for the possibility of their being quite different from those of the subject. The second alternative will not do as a condition for understanding because it presupposes too much. It seems to me that I must already have a very real understanding of the person concerned to enable me to become him, as it were. I must already know and understand what it is like to be him, the subject, before I can successfully experience his situation. This is an important ability within a personal relationship which enables one to get yet further insights into the other's experiences but it is, as it were, the end product of a deep understanding, not a condition of it.

A quotation from Collingwood, who lays stress on the notion of empathy, will help to make the issue more explicit:

Suppose . . . he (the historian) is reading the Theodosian Code, and has before him a certain edict of an emperor. Merely reading the words and being able to translate them does not amount to knowing their historical significance. In order to do that he must envisage the situation with which the emperor was trying to deal, and he must envisage it as that emperor envisaged it. Then he must see for himself, just as if the emperor's situation were his own, how such a situation might be dealt with; he must see the possible alternatives, and the reasons for choosing one rather than another; and thus he must go through the process which the emperor went through in deciding on this particular course. Thus he is re-enacting in his own mind the experience of the emperor; and only in so far as he does this has he any historical knowledge, as distinct from merely philological knowledge, of the meaning of the edict.[3]

Now, in order for the historian to envisage the emperor's situation as if it were his own, the historian must have a deep understanding of the emperor, one which he cannot obtain by indirect knowledge of him. Under the circumstances, the best he can do is to see himself in the situation and thus his analysis and judgments will be of a strongly subjective kind. This is in fact what Popper rightly, I think, objects to about this sort of account but his objection seems to be based on different reasons from the reasons I am offering. Since, however, his reasons have a direct bearing on what is involved in understanding persons, it would be useful, for my purposes, to digress somewhat and stay with this discussion.

Popper objects to the view that an analysis of a situation serves merely as an indispensable help to the re-enactment of the situation by the historian. His objection is based on the following reasons: He regards situational analysis as of prime importance and the psychological process of re-enactment as inessential and goes on to say:

. . . , though I admit that it may sometimes serve as a help for the historian, a kind of intuitive check of the success of his situational analysis. *What I regard as essential is not the re-enactment but the situational analysis.* The historian's analysis of the situation is his historical conjecture which in this case is a metatheory about the emperor's reasoning. Being on a level different from the emperor's reasoning, it does not re-enact it, but tries to produce an idealized and reasoned reconstruction of it, omitting inessential elements and perhaps augmenting it. Thus the historian's central metaproblem is: what were the decisive elements in the emperor's problem situation? To the extent to which the historian succeeds in solving this metaproblem, he *understands* the historical situation.[4]

Several important issues arise from this, issues which have a very direct bearing for my account of person understanding. First of all, in as far as Popper here speaks of *historical* explanation he is, I think, quite right in stressing what he takes to be the essence of historical explanation qua historical explanation. Where I think he goes seriously wrong is in insisting that by solving the metaproblem the historian then also has an understanding of the emperor, the individual. The latter, however, is not reducible to the former and I doubt whether we can get a proper grip of what 'understanding' in this area amounts to unless we look at this issue in a wider perspective. What Popper has to say in the historical context does, I think, reinforce my point, discussed in Chapter 1, about the serious inadequacy of his account of person understanding.

What should be stressed in the historian's case is that, quite contrary to Popper's willingness to admit that his re-enactment may serve as an intuitive check of the success of his situational analysis, such a check is ruled out in any historical explanation on the same grounds as I gave in the case of pen-friends. The historian, by having no direct knowledge and understanding of the emperor in question, is precluded from access to checks of any such kind; checks which are vital for an objective personal understanding (even if this is not objectivity as Popper demands it). All that is available to the historian is scientific evidence to support his explanation. For the same reason Collingwood's demand for re-enactment through empathy also fails. There is a very definite limit set here to the direction an explanation can take. At best, Collingwood's historian may base his explanation on how *he* would have reacted in a given situation because he has no access to the history of the emperor qua the person he was. Popper's historian who 'simply omits inessential elements' is blind to the complexities of what is involved in deciding what is inessential in this particular context. Without a real understanding of the emperor we cannot decide or even adequately understand what the inessential elements were for him except, of course, in the trivial case of what has no obvious connection.

These considerations show both Popper's very limited and limiting notion of what is involved in understanding another person and also the difficulties inherent in the concept of empathy. One element, however, is strongly implicit in and common to the issues raised above which I alluded to at the beginning of this discussion. Sympathy, antipathy, empathy and affinity all carry with them an appeal to feeling, they all point to the importance of some emotional component in personal understanding. I shall, therefore, discuss this aspect of understanding in detail. But first I have to return to the concept of affinity. It might be helpful to mention at the outset that I am not here concerned with any psychological aspects of what, I believe, is termed 'identification' which has, for me at least, implication of mirror images (seeing oneself in another as one takes oneself to be). The problem concerning the notion of affinity that I am particularly concerned with is that of its relation to what I have briefly mentioned in my first chapter, namely the question whether people who have the ability to understand others well possess certain extra concepts which not everyone has. I said that this suggestion, as it stands, seems to me, ex hypothesi, impossible to answer in general terms —if we lack these concepts then there is nothing we can say about them; if, on the other hand, we do possess certain of these concepts, we may be entirely unaware that we are applying them where others could not do so. One possible explanation may, perhaps, be offered here by tying the problem to the concept of affinity.

4.3 The Concept of Affinity

It might be useful to distinguish between two notions of affinity, one of which has already been discussed in detail in Chapter 2, where the explanation of affinity was focused on perceptual considerations. For the sake of clarity I shall refer to the two notions as affinity$_1$ and affinity$_2$. Affinity$_1$ is closely bound up with the Kantian notion that the experience of beauty in nature is hinting at an affinity between the noumenal self of the subject and that of external nature. Merleau-Ponty makes a very similar point in a more general context in that he holds that perception in the full-blown sense is possible only for a being which is of the same being as the things it senses. The individual is very much palpably in the world and a part of it and thus, most importantly, in an affinity with it. Knowledge and understanding are only possible when the subject and the things to be known or understood are thoroughly adapted to each other in an infinite relation of interaction based on affinity. In Kantian terms this amounts to saying that our knowing the world as we do is necessarily bound up with our sensibilities. Merleau-Ponty, in addition, sees this relation as all important for perception as it is dependent as much on the object as on the person perceiving it in the sense that the relation existing between them (in this case the subject and the world) is such that the spectator talks of himself in it as much as of it in him.

This account of perception is crucial when extended to apply particularly to our understanding of persons and the bringing out of the role affinity plays in this. The relation of interaction which is set up, with all its complexities, is that of the setting up of a situation in which both participants find themselves. The power in the one person to provide the other with certain experiences is a power to permeate that experience and invoke others connected with it; here it is not merely a question of noting any given features of behaviour by observation. Now, what experiences a person evokes in another is to a large extent dependent on the particular experiences undergone by the other. This is very much a creative process in which both perceiver and object cooperate; in my case it is the two persons concerned. The relation of inter-action discussed above now becomes a relation of reciprocity (in the context of persons).

The reciprocity which is set up between the two persons is very much dependent on the particular abilities, the degree of outgoingness they are capable of, and their experiences which are particular to the persons concerned and necessary as a basis for learning about the other and understanding the other. It is at this point that affinity$_2$ becomes important. So far, in our discussion of affinity$_1$, the main point was the general necessity for affinity between the knower and the knowable; between the perceiver and what is there which makes it possible to perceive. Affinity$_1$ is thus a necessary condition for knowledge and understanding both of persons and of material objects.

Affinity$_1$ is then a necessary community while affinity$_2$ implies interaction in a general sense—response and counter-response in turn. Affinity$_2$ plays a part in particular cases of person under-standing. What exactly it consists in can only be spelled out in detail with reference to particular cases. The responses and counter-responses are dependent on all sorts of considerations which are particular to the persons concerned, such as that of the complex conceptual web a person employs in perceiving, and this is also backed up by *his* particular knowledge and experience of persons. By this I mean that much of the interaction/reciprocity between two persons (what I understand and what the other evokes in me) is dependent on and stems from our past experi-ences, interests, dispositions, abilities and psychological make-up. Our experiences are a part of the very complex conceptual back-ground necessary to our understanding, which is also strongly influenced by the personal factors listed, and this involves more than subsuming a given aspect understood under a concept, of identifying it as a such and such. It also, often, involves the understanding of a given situation which is set up between two particular persons.

But often we try to understand a person—the subject—in a situation in which we are not involved. We try to understand from 'the outside', as it were. In such cases my understanding of the role I play in the relationship is not involved directly in my understanding of the subject's situation. Yet the degree of affinity I have with his situation will still be decisive to the degree of understanding possible on my part. The crucial point is that when we understand the situation, whether we are involved in it or whether we try to understand it as objects outside the subject's situation, the understanding is in terms of the present experience as well as against a background of past experiences. But our understanding will be limited to the extent to which we are capable of responding and counter-responding. There is, I think, an analogy here between the affinity involved in understanding persons and our ability to appreciate a joke. We may fail to see a joke, even though we understand what is being said, because we are unable to respond appropriately to the particular brand of humour. We respond negatively, as it were. Our sense of humour is not in affinity with the brand of humour of the joke.

Being a particular person involves a particular way of responding and understanding counter-responses. How we are able to interact in given situations is dependent on very complex factors which cannot be spelled out but our understanding on a personal level will be limited to the extent to which we are able to respond in an appropriate way—the understanding depends on an affinity of response and counter-response. This is an affinity which enables us to achieve reciprocity and recognition on a deeper level than simply that of identifying a situation as a such and such.

I have referred to the importance of our past experiences as bases to our understanding. This could be taken to imply a necessary community of background of two people between whom affinity$_2$ exists. I do not wish to imply this; I have explicitly made the point, in the previous chapter, that similar background experiences will affect various persons in different ways. My main point is that our experiences influence our becoming the sort of person we are and, to some extent, regulate what we are and are not capable of by way of responses. But, at the same time, it is important to note that the same experience may affect people

E

differently and thus a community of background experiences per se in no way implies affinity. It is rather how we extract what we find of importance that may result in affinity; how we respond to situations. My reference to experience in the context of affinity₂ is, nevertheless, mainly tied to the importance of past experiences as an influence on the sort of person one is—that is an issue quite separate from any notion of community of background. It is at this level that marked differences between persons become significant; if what we are able to extract from various experiences differs to a large extent, so will our understanding, that is, how we understand and, therefore, mutual understanding may become very difficult.

Whether our deep understanding of another involves having certain concepts others do not possess still seems to me to be a question which does not admit of an answer. What, I think, emerges from the above discussion is that we apply concepts which are backed up by our direct experience. But lack of experience or a significant difference in what two people are capable of extracting from an experience limits the degree of affinity between the persons concerned thus making the setting up of a reciprocal situation difficult.

It is at this point, I think, that Merleau-Ponty's thesis about external and internal horizons becomes very significant. As already mentioned, this thesis raises difficulties when applied to the perception of objects in general, as it is difficult to see what the interior horizons are where every object is concerned; or, to repeat the question I posed in this context—considering the intertwining at stake, it would be difficult to answer the question: 'An intertwining of us and what?' These particular difficulties disappear, however, when applied to the understanding of persons; both the notions of internal and external horizons and the intertwining which is necessary now make sense as Proust's example from *Swann's Way* so forcibly shows;[5] here the importance of affinity stemming from past and present experiences is clearly brought out.

The intertwining of the perceiver and the perceived entails, I think, the intertwining on both levels, i.e., both the exterior and the interior horizons, the interpretation of both being largely dependent on the particular situation which is set up between subject and object (two persons). The perceiver has to enter, as it were, into the dark interior horizons as well as take account of the exterior horizons of the words and expressions, i.e., the visible object confronting him; the two aspects are inseparable. It depends on his sensitivity what understanding will occur, whether he will be able to extract what is relevant; whether this is available to him.

As already suggested, Merleau-Ponty's ideas work in a most interesting way when applied to art; they also acquire very significant importance when applied to the understanding of persons. One of the powers inherent in art is to make our inner life yield up what lies hidden—our emotions and dispositions, the depth of response we are capable of, aspects of ourselves we are often not aware of. Such an awareness may come as a result of our reflexively apprehending our involvement with the work. It is, perhaps, interesting that the revelation is in most part of something positive about us. Art cannot reveal anything negative except, perhaps, a feeling of some fairly *general* lack—lack of response and the like. This is because to be aware of any *specific* lack presupposes our knowing positively whatever it is before we can realise that we are lacking it. The point I am making can be stated in rather familiar colloquial terms—one cannot miss what one never had, i.e., what one does not know about. However, our response to certain aspects of the given work (or lack of response) may be very revealing to others.

It seems to me that personal relationships and personal understanding perform the same role of revelation. The part affinity plays here could, perhaps, be described in terms of one person being able to strike the right chord in another who is also able to reciprocate and respond. Affinity becomes a kind of receptivity which leads to reciprocity as a creative process of understanding. I discover not only the other, but through my relationship with him my inner life is revealed to my understanding.

Both in the case of art and personal relationships the perceiver is provoked to use his understanding thus evoking a sensitive awareness. The power inherent in provoking the appropriate understanding in us is an objective power though dependent on our particular personal experiences which regulate what sort of understanding we are capable of. The concept of affinity in general is based on what one is capable of understanding, the sort of conceptual understanding that is supported by what lies within one's experience which not only enables one to enrich that conceptual understanding but, importantly, also acts as a limiting factor to the depths of understanding possible. These considerations arise from affinity$_1$ but in addition affinity$_2$ is, I think, a very important and basic condition for a closer understanding—a sort of being with the other in his world, as it were, in addition to just knowing about him from the outside. My failure to understand may be due on a simpler level to my not knowing enough about him, it may be due to my lack of sensitivity or imagination, but more significantly it may be because I find him too complex and quite outside my experience. The power in the other to provoke understanding will fail to find its mark, it just is not there to find. Conversely, I may fail in my attempt really to understand, however deep my interest, however rich my experiences, if the other does not wish it; for then any building up of receptivity and reciprocity becomes impossible, as it often does with people who are 'naturally' inscrutable.

I have given an account of the concept of affinity in rather general terms. This is because, it seems to me, the notion of affinity$_1$ lends itself to an explanation in general terms; it applies generally. The notion of affinity$_2$ comes into play most forcibly in particular cases. Any adequate account of the latter notion would have to consist of descriptions of interactions between two persons in various, particular cases. This is so, I think, because affinity manifests itself in many different ways and that is why I have so far merely hinted at some general factors inherent in the notion. I shall, in the next chapter, where I will be discussing particular cases of understanding, go some way towards showing, although implicitly, the part affinity plays.

4.4 The 'Power to Provoke' as a Creative Process of Understanding

I have strongly stressed the importance of the 'power to provoke' in the above account; its importance as a creative process is bound up with reciprocity. Here again we find a strong implication that there are emotional components in personal understanding, and these must now be dealt with. It is therefore necessary to take a closer look at what this power to provoke consists in or rather, perhaps, what gives rise to this power as a condition of real understanding within personal relationships. This brings me back to the problem raised at the beginning of this chapter: given that my distinction between different kinds or levels of understanding rests on different circumstances which allow the possibility of access to the objective and subjective aspects of a person's life, it is necessary to examine what these circumstances, which are conducive to provoking real understanding within a personal relationship, are. The problem turns on how different the circumstances have to be from those necessary for that understanding of a person's attributes or characteristics which I have already discussed. As I see it, there are really two separate, though closely related problems to which I must address myself:

1. Given the centrality of the notion of particular circumstances conducive to the development of the power to provoke as a creative process of understanding, what particular issues are involved here?

2. What is involved in the notion of 'power to provoke'—what does that power consist in?

I shall take these two related problems in turn.

A preference for scientific explanation of understanding persons on the grounds that it is uncluttered by personal attitudes and thus more likely to be correct, etc., amounts to construing knowledge of persons on the model of knowledge of material objects. This preference is also, as I suggested in Chapter 3, firmly rooted in, or rather stems from, an apprehension of the role which emotions play in personal relationships and an apprehension of being led into error by their very idiosyncratic nature. For while too close an emotional involvement may blind us to important aspects of another person's intentions or character, equally, an absence of any feeling precludes us from the closeness necessary for real understanding.

It seems to me that both scientific and personal knowledge allow of error but to prefer the former is to fail to allow for considerations arising from the sort of entity a person is. We are yet again confronted with the, by now, very familiar choice: science or art? I have already discussed in some detail the deep-rooted mistake inherent in an insistence on such a dichotomy in the context of person understanding. The last word on this issue must be that of the eminent psychologist Jerome Bruner whose answer to this question is subtle, impressive and utterly persuasive:

Reaching for knowledge with the right hand is science. Yet to say only that much of science is to overlook one of its excitements, for the great hypotheses of science are gifts carried in the left. . . .
And should we say that reaching for knowledge with the left hand is art? Again it is not enough, for . . . there is a barrier between undisciplined fantasy and art. To climb the barrier requires a right hand adept at technique and artifice. . . .[6]

To fail to take these considerations into account is to insist on a further misguided dichotomy between *what is to count* as rational and irrational. The dichotomy in question has at its roots the notion of the irrationality and therefore irrelevancy of the emotions based on their essential passivity.

I have raised a very large and complex issue and I cannot hope to do it justice within the scope of my topic; this would require a full-blown theory of the emotions. Instead, I shall try as concisely as possible to show why I take emotions to have an essential role in person understanding and why I think that a general dismissal of the important role emotions play in our understanding on the grounds of their passivity and irrationality cannot be justified. Thus the view which I think stands in need of serious questioning could be put in a very simplified way as follows: The mind is sometimes active and at other times passive. Activity of mind is associated with being rational, making choices, taking decisions, forming intentions, etc. Passivity of mind is associated with being passive in the sense of being caused by various phenomena and thus the opposite of active and rational—being irrational. Activity of mind is closely related to rational decision-taking whereas passivity being independent of one's decisions is irrational because caused independently of any deliberation on one's part.

I am not particularly concerned here with this account of the dichotomy of mind. My concern is with the next step which places emotions firmly in the latter category. Thus all emotions are taken as passive and therefore irrational. It is not at all clear why what is passive must also be irrational nor is it obvious that emotions are necessarily passive. As importantly, I do not see why one should insist that emotions do not involve any rational thought. It seems to me that they at least involve seeing things in certain ways and this requires the application of concepts or, more generally, thoughts which to some extent enter into attitudes, feelings and emotions.

I said that emotions involve seeing things in *certain* ways. This is because I do not want to rule out altogether any suggestion that our feelings or emotions are often caused in the sense that we all have predispositions to certain feelings which have a causal background and which may influence how we see things, what attitudes we have and to what extent we feel about things. In such cases, however, feelings and emotions stand to the perception in an internal relation. All perception of persons involves some attitude towards the other even if it is an attitude of disinterest, and it is therefore impossible to construe the seeing of a person in a certain way, such that the perception is separated off from the attitudes and feelings—they are, it seems to me, entirely inter-related. The notion of causation involved here will not serve to support the thesis that emotions are *necessarily* passive and therefore also irrational. Such an account does not cover all possibilities; it does not cover the ways in which our emotional attitudes, which are an essential part of our form of life, contribute to our understanding of central features of human life, features which, I suggest, could not be adequately understood independently of a connection with the emotions.

Persons, by virtue of being persons, stand in relationships with others and to understand a person is to understand something of the relationships in which he stands. By the very nature of such relationships, which are rich in all kinds of emotional attitudes, to try to give a purely intellectual account would be to blind oneself to important facts about our form of life.

We find throughout the history of philosophy a movement advocating the cultivation of purely rational, cognitive powers, this achievement being dependent on the suppression and eradication of emotions. There seem to be two separate issues arising from the above view. The first demands an answer to the question whether such a being would be superior to human beings as we know them. This must remain an open question but one could ask instead whether we could make sense of human agency without any reference to emotion concepts. Can we grasp as intelligible the notion of a calculating, conscious, rational, emotionless agent? It seems to me that his very 'agency' is immediately called into question because paradigmatically an agent engages in activities which to a lesser or greater extent he cares about and it is through such considerations that human actions and thus human beings are understood. Thus the second issue is that which raises the more important question for our purposes: Could such a being, a pure intelligence, be seen as a human being? The answer must, I think, be a firm 'no' because in an important way he would no longer be sharing in our form of life. Human beings are subject to emotions or feelings in ways which influence how they see and understand the world and other human beings in that world. Many of the central features of human life cannot be understood independently of a connection with the emotions. Nelson Goodman encapsulates some of the above issues in the following quotation:

The eye comes always ancient to its work, obsessed by its own past and by old and new insinuations of the ear, nose, tongue, fingers, heart and brain. It functions not as an instrument self-powered and alone, but as a dutiful member of a complex and capricious organism. Not only how but what we see is regulated by need and prejudice.[7]

The notion that emotions are passive, that they flood over us, overwhelm us and so on, is still strongly embedded in the Philosophy of Mind. It is difficult to see why this model of the emotions still has such a hold over various philosophers. Richard Wollheim, for instance, wonders why we are unaccountably transported by laughter on seeing something foolish or, again, as unaccountably, being thrown down.[8] It seems to me very curious indeed that he should be so puzzled. Up to a point he has already accounted for the laughter and let down in the very way in which he presents it as a problem. On seeing something funny or foolish, people, at least those with a sense of humour, will laugh but then there comes a point where, as we often say, enough is enough. This is just something that people do, amongst other things like speaking, sleeping, smiling at someone and so on. People who laugh for no reason (unaccountably) are people we begin to worry about. This example is just one vivid consequence of building a theory of emotions on their 'essential' passivity. We are at the mercy of what is capricious and irrational. Given this view it is, perhaps, no wonder that the role which emotions play in our understanding of others and of ourselves has largely, though not altogether, escaped philosophical scrutiny.

One reason for the neglect is a lack of awareness of the complexities involved in individual human emotions, a lack which is exhibited revealingly in the rather simplistic dichotomies which are thought to be appropriate here—active/passive and rational/irrational.

A good example is the, by now standard, analysis of jealousy. Jealousy is often cited as a paradigm of an irrational and/or immoral emotion. It is argued that loving someone entails, above all, a commitment to their happiness and this is incompatible with jealousy with its essentially egoistical element of possessiveness. Such a view of human emotions in general and jealousy in particular seems to me basically irrational; it completely fails to take into account what human beings really are like. The lofty sentiments expressed in the above argument are most appropriate to saints, martyrs or a very few, very exceptional human beings. We cannot ignore in any argument, in this context, how, in fact, *most* people feel. The argument is also too facile and too simplistic in failing to take into account different kinds of jealousy some of which could legitimately be condemned while others could be understood and sympathised with. Jealousy is never a pleasant or desired emotion.

But I wish to make a stronger claim: that loving someone without ever feeling jealous would throw in doubt the very genuineness or depth of the love felt. The criticism levelled at jealousy in terms of seeing the other person as something to be possessed is, I think, ill conceived. What is at stake here is that if a given relationship means 'everything' to me in the sense that it makes my life viable, influences the way in which I see the world, is precious to me, then anything that threatens it is quite naturally viewed with hostility and apprehension. It is my intense caring about the other person and about the relationship that makes me apprehensive and hostile to any factor that could adversely influence its continuance. If this is to count as possessiveness then surely it is so in a very special sense.

Alternatively, supposing someone claimed that his understanding of love has changed as a result of seeing that what he took to be a case of profound and devoted love has turned to jealousy. This just does not make sense and is indeed based on a misunderstanding of the relationship. One cannot be jealous about someone or something that one does not care about—this is both a conceptual and an empirical point. It is not the case, in the above example, that love turned to jealousy but that the relationship has changed, something has been added.

Thalberg, in his article 'Mental Activity and Passivity', discusses several well known philosophers who cling to this traditional imagery of the emotions. He asks whether emotions are passive and whether they indeed operate like surging floodwaters, ferocious winds, uncontrollable flames, unruly saddle-horses, or citizens rebelling against their government; they tug at us or propel us headlong, they overpower us. He offers a strong argument against the very possibility of categorising emotions as passive. He asks us to suppose that we are either victims or bystanders (the only two possible alternatives for a passive state) when emotions like shame, rage, lust or embarrassment invade our mind. He then poses the question: 'What could it possibly mean to say that these happenings constitute *our* shame, *our* fury, *our* craving . . .?'[9] He concludes that the bystander and victim models are useless for a very strong and clear reason. If someone is drenched by a cloudburst or kidnapped we would never say that it was the person's downpour or the person's kidnapping. These events have no owner since the individual's role in them is entirely passive. Thus, if I am a victim or a bystander when an emotion 'occurs' or comes over me, it could not make any sense to call it mine, in as much as I just happen to be 'in the way' or 'in its vicinity'. It becomes clear that neither of the two models make sense of the passivity of emotions let alone of the central role that emotions play in our lives.

In his summary, Thalberg writes:

The 'passivity' thesis in question seemed empty, since we could suggest nothing in the mental arena which might act upon us, in the clear-cut way that kidnappers act upon their prey. . . . Moreover, if we have a merely bystanding relationship to our emotions. . . , we shall be at a loss to explain what makes them 'ours'. . . .
Overall, we discovered no 'way . . . of determining the passivity or otherwise of our inner life'. . . . So until we encounter more compelling arguments for this distinction within the psychological realm,

I think we would avoid gratuitous mysteries if we confine activity and passivity to the physical world.

Thalberg is very aware of the point that emotions never *just* happen to us. They are connected with how we see things, what we care about, what matters to us—in short, there is a strong and necessary relation between our emotions, *ours* in the strongest sense, and the sort of persons we are. I shall try to examine the complex features of various emotions thereby attempting to establish their close relation with, and the crucial role they play in, our evaluation and understanding of persons. Very often a failure to feel an emotion is taken as revealing an absence of interest or insensitivity, or may result in moral condemnation, as in the case of learning of some outrage being committed where one ought to feel angry and indignant but does not; the 'ought' here is a moral 'ought'. We are condemning the person in question for his callousness, for being, what Thalberg calls, a passive bystander, instead of *reacting* to a situation in an emotionally appropriate way.

Any attempt to give an account of persons and person understanding independently of the emotional dimension must, as I shall argue, result in a distorted picture of what human beings essentially are. Collingwood's chilling and frightening description of the state of affairs depicted in Eliot's *Wasteland* dramatically underlines the consequences on the lives of human beings who no longer feel emotion.

The poem depicts a world where the wholesome flowing water of emotion, which alone fertilizes all human activity, has dried up. Passions that once ran so strongly as to threaten the defeat of prudence, . . . are shrunk to nothing. No one gives; no one will risk himself by sympathizing; no one has anything to control. We are imprisoned in ourselves, becalmed in a windless selfishness. The only emotion left us is fear; fear of emotion itself, fear of death by drowning in it, fear in a handful of dust.[10]

What I have said so far was merely an indication of how emotions contribute to and are essential in our understanding of others in a way that is rational and/or active. Since the distinction between active and passive rests mainly on rational decision-taking and being caused by various phenomena respectively, it would, therefore, be most useful for my purposes to examine what part, if any, our emotions have in rational decision-making and, further, whether the part they take is necessarily irrational. The question I want to raise is whether a person qua decider can be separated from and independent of his attachments, attitudes, relationships and emotions which I take to be a large part of the background from which the need for decision-taking stems, although not, perhaps, in all cases. It seems to me that our understanding, reactions and ways of seeing things and persons in certain ways cannot be neatly separated off into compartments of rational thought, belief, emotional factors and so on. In an important way there is a very significant interaction between them which I must now try to spell out.

Notes

1 Aristotle, *Nicomachean Ethics*, Book VIII, 1156a, 2ff.
2 H. T. Martineau, *Briery Creek*, 11.
3 R. G. Collingwood, *The Idea of History*, Oxford, 1946, p. 283.
4 K. R. Popper, *Objective Knowledge*, Oxford, 1972, p.188.
5 M. Proust, *Swann's Way*, trans. C. K. Scott Moncrieff, Vol. II, Pt. 2, Chatto & Windus, 1971, pp. 176-88.
6 J. Bruner, *On Knowing: Essays for the Left Hand*, Harvard University Press, 1962, p. 2.
7 N. Goodman, *Languages of Art*, Harvester Press, 1977, p. 7.
8 R. Wollheim, 'Expression', *Royal Institute of Philosophy Lectures*, Vol. I, Macmillan, London, 1968, pp. 272-44.
9 I. Thalberg, 'Mental Activity and Passivity', *Mind*, Vol. LXXXVII No. 347 (July 1978), pp. 393-5.
10 R. G. Collingwood, *The Principles of Art*, Oxford University Press, 1960, p. 335.

5 Emotions and Understanding

My main purpose is to bring out the central role which emotions and emotional concepts play in both self and other understanding thus attempting to argue that it is mistaken to treat of emotions as purely or necessarily or essentially passive phenomena which are therefore also irrational. The picture of a man which emerges from this view of emotions seems fraught with serious conceptual difficulties. On this view we are asked to regard emotions as something that happens to a creature who would be intelligible to us as a human agent quite independently of this important emotional dimension. This, however, is to presuppose that emotions are somehow not a part of what we take a person 'really' to be. I suggest, on the contrary, that such a view is based on a misunderstanding of the concept 'person'. Our reflections upon our past and present activities, involvements and reactive attitudes such as remorse, embarrassment, shame, regret, anger, love, satisfaction, joy and perhaps pride, are necessary for the conception of ourselves as persons. Similarly, the understanding of other persons without their historical background of this kind would be extremely difficult.

Without the above considerations it would be well-nigh impossible to come to grips with what would amount to an understanding of a particular person as a person of a certain kind. The development of one's understanding is at the same time very much a development in oneself, of the person one is, and this kind of understanding is not simply reducible to the perfection of a specialised skill. Emotions, I shall attempt to show, are closely related to the growth of understanding in that emotional attitudes, attachments and involvements are among the circumstances which enable situations to occur which aid such growth or development of understanding and, further, that those situations and the way a person deals with them must themselves be characterised in terms of some relevant emotion concepts; such concepts, in turn, have to be understood in terms of what their role is in the life of a human being who is both rational and capable of feeling emotions.

5.1 Appropriate and Inappropriate Emotional Responses

We are often afraid of showing our emotions on the grounds that we do not want to give ourselves away, to expose to others our subjective aspects, to show whom or what we really care about. This is very revealing in underlining the importance of emotions in our understanding of others in terms of their attitudes, of what is important to them, why they react in the way they do and what makes them vulnerable. Personal relationships of certain kinds, which encourage the growth of understanding, often do so by making the persons concerned less inhibited, less afraid or hesitant about revealing their feelings—all of which really amounts to a preparedness to give oneself away, to allow oneself to be oneself by getting involved in a personal relationship. Merleau-Ponty's discussion of the Schneider brain-damage case is very relevant:

Schneider, and the majority of impotent subjects, 'do not throw themselves into what they are doing'. . . . , and in so far as the subject coolly perceives the situation, it is in the first place because he does not live it and is not caught up in it. . . . Faces are for him neither attractive nor repulsive. . . . Sun and rain are neither merry nor sad; his humour is determined by elementary organic functions only, and the world is emotionally neutral. Schneider hardly extends his sphere of human relationships at all, and when he makes new friendships they sometimes come to an unfortunate end: this is because they never result, as can be seen on analysis, from a spontaneous impulse, but from a decision made in the abstract.[1]

It might be objected that my use of this example is not very illuminating because Schneider, by virtue of his brain damage, may also have been inhibited in his powers of reasoning and this was the reason for his inability to form any relationships; that is why in an important sense he could not be reached. But this objection, as it stands, misses the point of the example, namely that people's powers of reasoning generally involve some connection with spontaneous impulses tinged with emotional tones of interest, enthusiasm, warmth, responsiveness and the like; considerations which in Schneider's case were not simply inhibited but absent altogether. It is because of such considerations that our conception of a person as agent with intentions and desires becomes blurred unless we admit that emotional factors have to be allowed for. If we take as an example the detached man, the man who never loses his calm demeanour, in certain circumstances we would, I think, have grave doubts as to whether he really understood what was going on around him or happening to him; his calm demeanour might be grossly inappropriate to the situation. This brings out the internal relation between perception and feelings already mentioned. It is also important to note that we can and do make judgments about the rationality or irrationality of emotions. We do have standards of appropriateness in this context and we know what would count as a departure from such standards.

An irrational emotional response is judged as such in terms of its being an inappropriate reaction to an emotional situation which reveals an inability to cope with the situation. The response becomes over-emotional to an extent where a breakdown of rational thinking is clearly detectable. On the other hand, the man who never responds in any emotional way, any spontaneous way to any situation can also be seen as lacking something in an important sense, such that the lack raises serious doubts about whether he really understands the situation confronting him. Thus it would follow that we have to allow both for rationality and irrationality of emotions because we do have standards of appropriateness arising from the former, standards which enable us to make judgments about mistaken or inappropriate emotional responses which may, and often do, cloud our understanding. Where our understanding is so clouded we need to take a more detached view of the situation, but this does not or need not imply a completely unemotional view.

A note of qualification is necessary here. When I speak of standards of appropriateness, I do not wish to imply that we have generally agreed criteria for *the* appropriate emotional responses in general. Such criteria would have to stem from the notion of conscious, rational agents from whom would derive standards of what it was appropriate to believe and therefore what attitudes would be appropriate. One such attempt is, I take it, made by Terence Penelhum. He writes:

One can judge an emotion as appropriate or inappropriate to its
object, as understandable, as disproportionate, and so on. To decide
whether someone's emotion is justified or not in these ways, one must
examine the cognitive core of it. . . . An emotion may be unjustifiable
because its cognitive core is false, i.e., if the facts are not as the person
having the emotion assumes them to be. It may, further, be unjustified
because it is inappropriate to the facts as the subject has understood
them. This is very complex. . . . That we judge certain emotions to be
fitting, and certain others not, suggests that we have a rough scale with
emotions, as it were, paired off against certain sorts of situations.[2]

Now, it seems to me, this is too simplistic a move. It suggests
something like: Let us look at a certain type of situation which is
a possible object of an emotion and set against this the emotional
response of the person concerned; thus will we be in a position to
judge the appropriateness or otherwise of that response. This
view presupposes, rightly, the generality of suitable objects of
emotions and appropriate or inappropriate types of response. In
so far as standards of appropriateness and inappropriateness are
tied to meaning which emotions have, we certainly have criteria
for judging emotional responses as justified/unjustified, suitable/
unsuitable, appropriate/inappropriate. I mean that, generally, we
can, for instance, point out to someone that his feeling proud
about x is unjustified since he had nothing to do with bringing
about x, on the grounds that the concept of pride involves considerations, arising from its meaning, about the sort of situations
one can and cannot be proud of. But Penelhum's view also implies
and presupposes the generality of the appropriateness/inappro-
priateness of scale of response.

The problem of judging, e.g., the appropriate intensity of a
particular response is tied to the problem how the specific
situation is to be understood and is not to be solved in terms of
pairing off certain situations and the emotional responses of the
person concerned. A situation cannot be seen in toto as a mere
repetition of a type to which solely general principles can be
applied. In addition our reliance on our judgment about what is
appropriate to a given situation has to be seen in terms of this
judgment arising from, or being supported by, our background
and our experiences of various situations.

But what I take to be the crux of the difficulty here is that my
understanding of the object of a given person's emotion is not

just seeing it as a suitable object for the emotion in general but a suitable object *for him.* We cannot make judgments about the appropriateness/inappropriateness of *the scale* or intensity of someone's emotional response without understanding much of his historical background. Thus, in addition to the pairing off of a given situation with a person's response, as Penelhum suggests, we must also consider the person concerned in the light of his past experiences.

Although there exists a degree of generality of suitable objects of emotions and appropriate/inappropriate types of response, there is no such principle of generality regarding *scales* of response. The deciding factor in this kind of understanding of an object of emotion is, I think, exactly similar to the account I gave of what is involved in understanding a situation: i.e., that features of a given person's background, past life, his experiences and interests are among the important conditions which will have to be taken into account in our understanding of what an appropriate degree of response would be in his case.

It seems to me that taking account of such conditions is not a matter of extracting criteria of appropriateness, which imply a degree of generality, but rather, as I have suggested, of taking cognisance of these conditions as vital for our understanding. From this background will arise the standards of appropriateness for the given case, so that we understand why, and thus understand that, his response to the object of emotion is an appropriate response, is suitable to the object as suitable for him. These standards, however, have to have public significance. In other words, we cannot understand what standards of appropriateness to apply independently of understanding what is appropriate to the life of a given person who not only feels the emotion but whose emotions and desires are influenced by his past relationships, past involvements and the conflicts which he has experienced and which influence his understanding.

What a person is capable of seeing in a situation and how he sees it is informed by his past history and thus the kind of understanding he brings to it; what he will consider particularly relevant will stem from the understanding which he has developed, from the ways he has of thinking about the world and his particular human relationships. Thus notions of appropriateness/ inappropriateness in this sense involve more than judgments based on applying general principles. To really understand a given person's response which seems at first glance out of proportion in some way, one has to understand the person himself.

That we need some degree of involvement in, interest in, enthusiasm for or caring about our activities is directly related to the meaningfulness human activities have; our interests, enthusiasm for, etc., act as a spur or motive for actions, but what endows actions with meaningfulness in this sense is the recognition that all these spurs or motives are to varying degrees emotion impregnated and not at all exclusively rationally, just decided upon.[3] The matter is not simply one of finding a rationally acceptable and appropriate object of activity, concern, involvement, interest or attachment; this procedure amounts to finding good reasons for one's actions but such well considered actions lack the spur which emotional involvement provides. The emotional dimension enables one to come to see activities in a different light, to care enough to want to do them in addition to having good reasons for doing them (although, I think, 'the good' here may already be loaded with emotional considerations).

Caring about, being involved, having certain emotionally charged attitudes towards certain activities, responses and the like, is what makes possible the exercise and engagement in those activities; what decides the kind of engagement in them. This kind of engagement stands in sharp contrast to activities stemming from indifference or prudence. Activities stemming from, e.g., indifference are most often described as 'mechanical', implying mere automatic movement, characterised in terms of physical occurrences which are, in an important way, external to the agent.

5.2 Spontaneous Actions in Relation to Emotions as Rational or Irrational

These points can, perhaps, be made clearer by reference to a person's spontaneous, undeliberated actions. At the root of the view I am questioning is the assumption that a man's detached, deliberated judgments are necessarily more appropriate because rational and, therefore, better in terms of the sort of criteria one uses to evaluate judgments; better than what a person is inclined to do or say as a result of his feelings and emotions, actions which are seen as spontaneous and undeliberated responses. It is in fact a view encapsulated in the admonitions to 'Stop and think', or 'Look before you leap.'

R. S. Peters, for instance, holds that some interference with reason is implied by the very description of a reaction as emotional.[4] He argues that the emotions get in the way of the exercise of one's rationality, partly on the grounds that someone whose reactions were emotional would not have acted in accordance with some calculation of means to an end, and that consequently such actions could hardly count as actions, mainly because the judgment involved would be wild and intuitive. He goes on to say that if a judgment is an expression of an emotion this implies a very poor judgment; emotions are 'mists on our mental windscreen'.[5] These remarks dismiss a whole range of emotion tinged actions as not being actions in the full sense. For instance, any spontaneous action or certain actions done for their own sake do not qualify as actions because in such cases, characteristically, there is no calculation of means to an end. Yet in such cases situations are perceived as given and acted upon—the perception of the given situation is then related to feelings or emotions on which one acts. Peters himself writes: 'The relationship between what a man sees a situation as and his emotional reaction to it is so close that it is plausible to suggest that the relationship is an internal one.'[6] Thus, it would follow that, given such an internal relation as long as an object of emotion can be seen as appropriate to a given person, to the kind of person he is, we must rule out, in any such responses, the judgment of them as necessarily irrational, as necessarily clouding reason or interfering with one's rational judgment.

An objection might be raised that I am not being altogether fair to Peters because he modifies the above view in his later works, e.g., his paper 'Reason and Passion'.[7] I must, therefore, consider this article in order to meet the possible objection. He writes that he wishes to show that what is often called 'the life of reason' is not inconsistent with a life of passion. This statement seems, on first reading, to be diametrically opposed to what he has to say in the earlier article. It is, therefore, necessary to make clearer to what extent the views expressed in the two articles differ and what the notion of passion implies.

Peters makes certain important distinctions which I shall attempt to summarise:

1. The behaviour of children and animals cannot be judged as reasonable/unreasonable, rational/irrational, because they lack the ability to reason in the sense of explicitly employing generalisations and rules in the forming of beliefs and in planning actions. They also lack what Peters takes as the second necessary condition—the employment of the concepts of past and future and thus 'the most general characteristic of reason which is the transcendence of the particular', the transcendence of the this, the here and the now. He then goes on to stress the objective character of reason which is irreconcilable with egocentricity and arbitrariness. One could ask here, as already argued, whether creative and interpretative thinking is not often egocentric at least to some significant degree.

2. Passions are intimately connected with the use of reason; they are not distinct entities that are liable to be mistaken for reason. The use of reason is inexplicable without passions. Peters writes:

Without *the attitude of impartiality,* for instance, the individual could not concentrate on relevant considerations and counteract his inclination to favour his own point of view or that of someone to whom he might be attracted or attached. . . . For to use one's reason is *to be influenced by this type of passion.*[8] (My italics.)

Peters abandons the distinction between calm passions which are associated with reason and turbulent passions 'of a less disinterested kind' on the grounds that one's *passion for truth* may be anything but calm. Now, in so far as the relation between perception and feeling is an internal one, so far are passions in Peters' sense intimately connected with reason.

3. There is a distinction between the philosophical and the 'ordinary' sense of 'passion'. Peters asks the following: 'And is there necessarily any contrast between reason and these *states of mind* (passions)?' I do not think that for Peters there is any real contrast. The passage which follows is important and I quote it in full:

A clue to this may be provided by asking when a passion, in the philosophical sense, would normally be referred to as a passion in ordinary language. When, for instance, would a concern for fairness or an abhorrence of irrelevance be referred to as a passion? Usually, surely, when looking at a situation in a way which warrants the term 'fair' or 'irrelevant' is connected with things that come over us, which we may not be able to control. To have a passion for truth suggests more than just caring about it. It suggests that we are strongly affected by disregard of evidence, inaccuracy and deceit. We are subject to strong feelings if truth is disregarded in any way. This links the use of 'passion' with the Latin *patior* from which it is derived. It suggests being subject to something, being mastered or overpowered. Hence the connection in ordinary language between passion and turbulence; for it is often, though not always, the case that when we are affected in this way our state of mind is a turbulent one.[9]

Peters allows a close connection, where passions are concerned, a connection in the sense of being affected and being disposed to act.

4. 'Unreasonable' behaviour differs from 'irrational' in that the agent has reasons for what he does but these are weak and he does not pay attention to the reasons of others. In such cases the man falls down 'on the cardinal requirement of objectivity'. 'Unreasonableness' has social dimensions which are not implicit in 'irrationality'. In a footnote to this discussion Peters writes: 'I have assumed that, in the case of actions, "unreasonable" and "irrational" are judgments passed on conduct in relation to *some end in view*.'[10] He goes on to say that we can judge ends as unreasonable but not as irrational. What we call emotions are good examples of passive states and we speak of emotions as being both unreasonable and irrational. He writes:

Some philosophers have held that all such transitory emotions are unreasonable, if not downright irrational. . . . Such a philosopher might therefore say that falling in love with anyone is quite irrational; for it involves becoming attached to a particular person in the world, ... We, on the other hand, might not see *the state of mind* in this cosmic context. We might regard falling in love as a-rational, just one of those things to which human beings are subject. Being in such a state would not qualify for being either reasonable or rational; for it would be denied that there are any standards of appropriateness by reference to which it could be judged. But, on the other hand, it *might* have little to do with passion either. For we might be *little moved by it*. Some impulses and inclinations might also fall into this category. Someone might just like looking at trees or at animals. Such a want might be neither reasonable nor unreasonable, and it might be so feeble that to call it a passion would also be a misnomer.

It does not seem, therefore, that the passive states, which we call emotions, are *necessarily* either irrational or unreasonable. Nevertheless there is a tendency for them to be. For as the appraisals, which are intimately connected with them, are of situations which are very important to us, they are often made rather intuitively and urgently, with little careful analysis of the grounds for making them. They are also the most potent *source* of irrationality in that attention to features which are relevant to making *other* sorts of judgments is often deflected by irrelevant appraisals which are conceptually connected with our emotions. . . . There is thus a much closer connection between being irrational and emotion than there is between emotion and being un-reasonable.[11] (My italics.)

Finally, I wish to quote a passage which is, perhaps, most significant for my purposes: 'Emotions, usually of a gusty sort, are aroused only by particular people and situations. Spinoza's account of the state of human bondage is a good description of this level of life.'[12] What then are the points of difference between these two articles? It is immediately obvious, I think, that the thesis about actions which are to count as actions still demands that actions must be done in accordance with some calculation of means to an end. This is brought out again and again via his two necessary conditions of employing generalisations and rules in the planning of actions and the employment of concepts of past and future, the transcendence of the this, the here and the now. These are necessary conditions for high-grade actions—absence of them results in low-grade life and thus in a life of bondage. Thus my point that there is no room in Peters' account for con-sidering as rational spontaneous actions, undeliberated actions and actions done for their own sake (since each and every action or activity must have a point), still stands.

5.3 Emotions and Passions

It is important to clarify possible distinctions or relations between passions and emotions. One vital point emerges—passions are states of mind. Thus, e.g., love which in Peters' view is a-rational, because we have no criteria for standards of appropriateness by reference to which it could be judged, also qualifies as a state of mind. I am not at all clear what standards of appropriateness are at stake here. Surely it is often quite rational to feel love towards another human being, and by extension of usage, towards a given work of art or even some particular, favourite object. Perhaps his point about appropriateness is bound up with cases where we often say 'I don't know what he sees in her'. This remark is not necessarily a result of a lack of standards of appropriateness as such; it is often tantamount to saying that we do not understand enough about what is involved in the given relationship.

Peters goes on to say that love may have little to do with passion 'for we might be little moved by it'. In one sense love may have little to do with passion but not in Peters' sense. The few examples which he explicitly gives of cases of passion are an attitude of impartiality, a passion for truth, the commitment to reason and objectivity which reason demands. The important question, it seems to me, is how the commitment to someone one loves is related to the commitment to truth? Commitment to truth seems to involve the notion of a principle one chooses to live by or spend one's life *pursuing*. I do not think that loving someone could be construed in any such way. Passions, in Peters' sense, are states of mind which involve what I would call an intellectual commitment. Emotions, on the other hand, or what we usually take to be emotions, may be states of mind in so far as they have a cognitive core but, in addition, they involve an experience which affects, in most cases, both body and mind. Many emotions are characteristically such that they develop or wane. I do not see how, e.g., an attitude of impartiality could affect one in the same way as, say, the experience of joy, fear, jealousy, pride and so on. Emotions are primarily directed towards other persons or evoked in others by us. Passions, in the ordinary sense, are primarily directed towards ideals or things—for justice, for truth, for an academic way of life or for cream cakes. Characteristically one pursues one's passions.

Peters himself says: 'Emotions of a gusty sort are aroused only by *particular people and situations*.'[13] But he adds that the state of human bondage is a good description of this level of life. 'This level of life' is here a low-grade level and, therefore, on his own account irrational. Thus the points which were made at the beginning of this discussion still hold, with one apparent exception: Actions must be performed in accordance with some calculation of means to an end; spontaneous, undeliberated actions cannot count as rational, because the judgment involved would be wild and intuitive (in the first version), or intuitive and urgent with little careful analysis of the grounds for making it (in the second version). Actions performed for their own sake do not count as actions unless their point is clearly recognised. The apparent exception centres on the phrase 'emotions are mists on our mental windscreen'. Here Peters skims off certain emotions which qualify as states of mind while the remainder (emotions of the gusty sort) qualify as irrational. 'There is . . . a closer connection between being irrational and emotion than . . . between emotion and being unreasonable.'[14] I am not sure what the distinction between rational *turbulent* and irrational *gusty* amounts to. In the later article, it is not the case that emotions are simply mists on our mental windscreen. In addition, in Peters' own words:

. . . it is simple-minded to analyse the situation in terms of dispassionate judgment being clouded by emotion. What we have is *not only* the presence of passions which sidetrack the individual and lead to distortion of judgment. . . . We have *also* the absence or weakness of passions which help the individual to keep his eye on the ball.[15]

The apparent exception, referred to above, hangs on the point that in the later article Peters discusses *in addition* a lack of passion and it becomes fairly clear, I think, that there is a difference between passions and emotions as these terms are normally used.

If there is a distinction to be made between passions and emotions it is that the former are paradigmatically directed towards material objects, virtues or ideals whereas the latter are directed towards people and situations. Passions are paradigmatically a-personal; sexual passions as such are in an important way, often, impersonal or a-personal, i.e., often referred to as 'purely physical'. Emotions, on the other hand, are primarily personal— directed towards a particular person *because* of the kind of person he is. I think that it is quite compatible to argue that a given person has a consuming passion for impartiality and at the same time maintain that the part emotion plays in his life is very insignificant.

The passion for always being dispassionate in one's understanding or judgment of others is not only impossible to maintain, but would be utterly inappropriate in one's relationships with other people. Nor do I think that egocentricity is necessarily incompatible with rationality. I wish at this point to offer some examples of judgments and actions arising *directly* from emotional reactions where such reactions and the understanding which follows cannot be seen as in any way irrational.

One such example can, I think, be established by asking the question whether one's being profoundly moved by a musical work and as a result judging the work as one of great artistic merit or beauty is *never* to count as a valid aesthetic judgment? Very often we can communicate more effectively by describing the work as it appears to us, expressing or showing our feelings without actually describing it. But when we describe our feelings, we must also be able to indicate or describe the relevant passages of the work. Communicating an aesthetic experience is never simply a matter of reporting our feelings—'This music makes me feel very sad'—but also of assisting someone else to perceive and respond to the work as we do. It is a question of referring feelings to parts of the work. At the same time, to fully experience aesthetically, say, Mahler's *Kindertotenlieder* it isn't appropriate simply to recognise the sad character of the music without ever being made sad by it. It is important to note that our mood of the moment cannot influence or change the mood of the music; the influence works in the opposite direction. Our mood, at most, will influence the adequacy or otherwise of our aesthetic response. At the root of aesthetic appreciation lies the ability to receive what the music has to offer. This is often a spontaneous reception which becomes a central part of the aesthetic experience as opposed to bringing to it too much analysis, too many preconceived ideas which may seriously impair our ability to receive what the music has to convey.

The importance of spontaneity can also be shown in reference to certain actions. As mentioned above, Peters insists that spontaneous, undeliberated actions cannot count as rational because the judgment involved is 'wild and intuitive'. Actions performed for their own sake do not count as actions unless their point (end) is clearly recognised; unless some calculation of means to an end takes place.

By direct contrast, S. I. Benn argues that an autonomous, rational man would not make a conscious decision before every action, nor a conscious deliberation of means to an end. Anyone trying or wishing to decide and deliberate to this extent, in Benn's words:

. . . would be an existentialist gone mad or would be suffering from a neurotic anxiety about doing the wrong thing. Most of the autonomous man's actions would be appropriate but non-deliberate responses to situations falling into fairly standard, readily recognisable categories.[16]

He does not say what the position would be in situations which do not fall into what he calls fairly standard categories but the implication is clear—that only in fairly out of the ordinary situations would a man need to deliberate and make conscious decisions. The point which is relevant here is that cases of conscious decisions cannot be equated with deliberations of means to ends. It seems to me that a person can and often does decide to act where the decision and action are almost simultaneous, but neither of these implies a deliberation of means to an end as a necessary condition for an action to count as rational. Insisting that some calculation of means to an end is essential to something's being seen as an action leaves out of account a whole dimension of activities done for their own sake, such as actions arising purely from one's love for another and constituting an expression of this love. Such actions cannot be dismissed as not full-blown actions on the grounds that we cannot spell them out in terms of calculating means to an end; similarly for moral actions or activities which one sees as worthwhile which are done for their own sake and not as means to ends. The means/end dichotomy does not apply here yet such activities cannot be seen as somehow falling short of what is to count as an action in the full sense.

Two objections may be raised here: that the means/end dichotomy I have used is different from *calculating* means in order to achieve x successfully and that moral actions are done out of one's passion for morality. But I don't think these objections will do because, firstly, in the cases quoted there is no means/end dichotomy as such. We are here concerned with in-

tentions to act in a certain way; ends do not enter into consideration. Secondly, I wish to include all kinds of actions, including
spontaneous actions arising from emotional responses which do
not necessarily stem from any passion. One could, of course,
produce an end in explanation here, saying, e.g., that acting
morally is an attempt to achieve the end of promoting the
maximum good in the world. But this is a rather artificial and
forced account of ends in the context of human actions and their
judgments. I rather suspect that one could also produce some such
end for spontaneous actions arising from emotional responses
(which would normally also be unconscious), such as that it was
done in order to cultivate one's natural humanistic instincts which
enrich one's life and that of others thus preventing human relationships from becoming quite sterile. Either account is too
simple and too forced.

In both cases this would be at best an account of the formation
of such responses, not their intentional end. Instead, I suggest,
we have to look to the role of emotional reactions in the context
of the whole network of human activities and reactions, and the
role they play specifically in our understanding of others towards
whom they are directed. It is on the strength of the above considerations that we can be in a position to decide and make judgments about the respect in which emotions belong to the subject's
passivity and the respect in which they possess an active character.
This way of going about deciding the issue highlights these
notions as important aspects of our thoughts about persons and
how we see persons in situations.

5.4 Emotional Responses and Understanding

Shared practices and shared activities are basic and necessary to
the development of human powers and to the development of
rationality. We can only understand what it is to be involved in
a given practice or activity via the conceptual network which has
been developed within the framework of inter-personal influences.
It is through such influences that we also come to care about
certain activities more than others; they become more personally
important. We develop loyalties, we feel contempt for others who
only dabble in them and fail to realise their importance, so that
our whole understanding of what is going on is largely dependent

on our feelings, our degree of caring about a given activity. Our understanding here cannot be separated from emotional factors, factors which are not in any real sense like Peters' rational passions.

Our emotions very often arise from the way in which we see a given person in a situation, how we understand the situation in terms of what confronts us. All these factors are to a large extent based on rational considerations, but our degree of caring or involvement will influence our judgments about the person's response to the situation and our feelings about his response may produce valuable insights.

A strict dichotomy between our concepts and beliefs about the world and our interests and ways of living in it is mistaken because the two are generally inseparable where our understanding is concerned. There is an all important connection between a person's passivity and his activity. This can be characterised in terms of the way in which a person's feelings and emotions are inter-connected with the *kinds* of activities and relationships he engages in and which provoke his growth of understanding of these. To what extent a person becomes involved in his activities and relationships depends, in large part, on the kind of emotional responses he will have to them. This is important both for other and for self understanding.

It is a fact that very often men will not allow themselves to act on immediate, generous impulses, following instead what might be termed a policy of non-involvement, through a cool calculation of advantages and disadvantages, of what can reasonably be expected of them, of the outcome of their actions or the possible degree of success. I do not wish to deny that such considerations are extremely important. What I have been disputing is the view that such actions are necessarily *always* more appropriate. Cases where such actions are, on the contrary, inappropriate cover a wide range of human situations. To what extent is it appropriate, for instance, to stop or control an inclination to help or relieve someone's suffering by allowing the intervention of deliberations based on considerations that 'I don't want to get involved' or 'Let him fight his own battles'? One cannot always follow the inclination, however strong, to act spontaneously because this would demand a degree of involvement which would seriously interfere with the viability of one's own life; but at the same time too much deliberation accompanying every wish to act would result in an inability to take any decision in extreme cases. On a lesser level this could be compared with too much rewriting and revision of a paper one has written where in the end the original thought may get blurred by too much exaggerated attention to detail; one may achieve an elegance of style at the cost of interest or even intelligibility. More importantly, there are many cases in which *the only* response is an immediate and spontaneous one, such as in cases of accidents, seeing someone in immediate need of help and such like.

Those kinds of cases are also extremely important within personal relationships where, say, as a result of the way in which one sees a given relationship, one approaches the other for advice or help and is met with a reaction which involves a hesitation instead of an immediate response. The failure to respond provokes questioning. There may, of course, be various reasons for this failure. But one may in some cases come to understand that such a response is not appropriate to the given relationship or that one's understanding of the given relationship was mistaken. The fact that the response was not what was expected may result in certain cases in a breakdown of the conception of that relationship. Typically, people who are unable to respond spontaneously in certain situations are people whom we see as incapacitated in an important way, in a way which prevents them from forming personal relationships.

I said just now that a person's understanding of his activities and of others is largely dependent on the kind of emotional response he has to them and that these points are equally important to the understanding of the self. This implies that there is no significant dichotomy between the understanding of the self and the understanding of others; it seems to me that this implication is correct. In both self and other understanding the power to provoke understanding is an emotional power which provokes questions leading to a deeper understanding in the same way that one of the powers of art is to reveal to us what lies hidden in our emotional life. Here again, art and music provoke questions about the emotional content of one's aesthetic experience—questions about why one is moved by a particular passage in a way which may lead to a deeper understanding of aspects of the work of art. The same applies to situations in which one finds oneself with others.

One may try to understand one's attitudes in terms of what it is about the person towards whom one feels drawn, or in whom one becomes interested and so on, and, further, why one finds certain features of a person's way of living attractive or repulsive which may in turn reveal to our understanding something of our own dispositions. There is much that manifests itself about a person and he can reveal it to himself by such questioning. In becoming aware of the need for questioning of his responses, he begins to learn to understand important things about himself. In one's relationships with others such questioning may often reveal an important truth about the relationship, a truth which conflicts with how one has viewed the relationship. Such emotion-provoked reflections may revise one's conception of the relationship, the need for the revision being compelled by one's emotional reactions which, if ignored, may lead one to self-deception or complete misunderstanding.

One cannot dismiss such important aspects of one's relationship with another simply on the grounds of the irrationality of the emotions. It seems to me that what would be irrational would be to ignore rather than question the object of such reactions.

In personal relationships, a person may find that he is involved in or has formed an attachment which he no longer wishes to continue on grounds that he now sees it as a strain charged with a whole range of emotions such as irritation, hate, sadness, resentment, and yet he cannot rid himself of that emotional involvement. This may be seen as a typical conflict between the dictates of reason and the irrational pull of emotions because he is unable to rid himself of emotions he now sees as undesirable, hopeless or whatever the case may be in a particular situation. Here again, however, reflecting on what it is that makes him unable to break off the relationship may reveal to his understanding some basic needs, for example, which, in spite of accompanying difficulties, the other person is able to fulfil; understanding how the person is able to fulfil an important need is also closely bound up with a real understanding of that person.

The important aspect of understanding here is one's realisation that it is not simply one's intentions and conscious decisions which reveal the sort of person one is but those involvements which go contrary to or are independent of one's conscious decisions and intentions, those which are not necessarily under one's control.

Similarly, the way one feels in the presence of another may be an important factor in understanding that person and oneself better. Such feelings again raise questions about what it is that makes one react in such a way thus enabling one to understand something about the other, some aspect which causes this reaction; one tries to arrive at a more detailed and precise description of what is going on. The point I am trying to stress is that our reactions and attitudes towards others, although emotional, are in an important way thought provoking and thus belong centrally to the understanding persons have of each other and of the self. Far from being seen as disruptions, a person's emotions should rather be seen as revealing in all kinds of ways; emotions often provoke deeper understanding.

Cases of conflict and emotional commotion such that the subject complains that he does not know what to think or how to act cannot be discussed simply in terms of interruptions in a man's rational life. They may be such interruptions but they could nevertheless come to fulfil an important and vital role in provoking the person concerned to face the situation he finds himself in, to come to grips with an attempt to identify the problem for what it is and in the course of such confrontation to come to understand what it is he really cares about, what matters to him, how he sees his activities and relationships. This, in turn, may lead to a questioning of a given relationship and an attempt to see it under different descriptions—all of which may lead to a better or deeper understanding. Emotional reactions which one feels towards another may force one to reassess one's understanding of the other, whereas a dismissal of such reactions as irrelevant may force one to persist in what amounts to self-deception both about the other person and the relationship. This sort of consideration becomes important in the sphere of moral assessments of relationships where one sees a response as morally undesirable or downright immoral and therefore wishes to repudiate the response.

Repudiating or ignoring such a response, or trying to deny its existence because, e.g., it is irrelevant to one's actions amounts to a deliberate blinding of oneself to important aspects of the self and the other. But this in itself is a complex ethical issue which I cannot pursue here.

A person's self understanding develops within his actual relationships with others from which deep satisfaction or problems and conflicts arise. His mere introspection of his own feelings in this context will yield, at best, theoretical deductions which cannot be falsified independently of the activities within the given relationship, or independently of reactive attitudes, spontaneous responses and what is said, all of which are manifested in those relationships and where reflection on them must make constant reference to the other in the relationship. This issue is exactly similar to the example I gave in Chapter 3—deep understanding between two people who correspond with each other but have never met is impossible because the vital theory/practice relationship which provides an independent check and standards of correctness is not present.

Our theoretical introspection separated from feelings arising within the interactions taking place within a relationship is not, by itself, adequate to self understanding. An examination of my own, inner feelings, which is independent from the activities within a relationship, is too subjective a matter and thus is inadequate for any real understanding of the self. How I react to the hopes, feelings, successes and failures of others forms an important part of self understanding in addition to how they react to me. Introspection which relies on taking a detached view, in a sense which involves stepping back from the relationship, as opposed to thinking about reactions which arise within the relationship during the interaction, cannot yield real understanding. Detached thinking implies seeing the self and the other as objects of contemplation and this leaves out considerations arising from live activities and reactions.

If we accept the importance of these considerations then emotions cannot be seen simply as exclusively and essentially passive phenomena. At best, it could be maintained that they possess a passive aspect in that we cannot command ourselves to feel or cease to feel an emotion. The same applies to the view that emotions are essentially irrational. It has, I hope, been shown that they are irrational only in so far as they are tied to the uncontrollable aspect of passivity just mentioned; they may, therefore, be irrational in some cases but not in those which I have discussed, where they lead to a deeper understanding. The view which ties certain or all emotions to some necessary interference with reason stems, I think, from a decision to give an account of emotions in terms of their necessary characteristics. But emotions include such a varied assortment of feelings that to speak in terms of some essential characteristic seems to me to be misguided. We get a mistaken view of their essential characteristics by selecting homogeneous examples of emotions and this practice is, to say the least, grossly misleading.

I have discussed the role emotions play in our understanding in terms of trying to answer the question whether a person qua decider can be separated from and be independent of his attachments, attitudes, relationships and the emotions which enter into these. It seems to me that emotions, although not themselves something that is decided upon, do illuminate, in the sorts of ways discussed, our decisions on how to act and when the need to act arises. They influence our decisions about how we are to understand or see the world and persons we come into contact with. My attempts to show why I take emotions to have a vital role to perform in our personal understanding served also to spell out the particular circumstances conducive to the development of the power to provoke a deep understanding seen as a creative power based on reciprocity.

The reciprocity in question is also important where understanding of the self is concerned in that such understanding is closely bound up with one's relationships and thus the understanding of others. One's understanding of the self and of others develops not only through the use of language and thinking, not only through an exchange of confidences or discussion of problems and common interests but, as importantly, in seeing and feeling the reactions and responses of others in given situations. The power which provokes real understanding here is the emotional power which illuminates and reveals to our understanding what may otherwise remain hidden. All these factors modify or greatly influence one's own understanding of situations, sometimes in very subtle ways, such that they cannot even be formulated in language.

I have repeatedly hinted above that the dichotomy which is sometimes set up between self understanding and the understanding of others is, at least in many cases, a false one. It is now necessary, in conclusion, to argue for this position explicitly.

F

5.5 The Relation between Self and Other Understanding

Hegel opens the Introduction to the *Philosophy of Mind* with the following paragraph:

The knowledge of Mind is the highest and hardest, just because it is the most 'concrete' of sciences. The significance of that 'absolute' commandment, *know thyself*—whether we look at it in itself or under the historical circumstances of its first utterance—is not to promote mere self-knowledge in respect of the *particular* capacities, character, propensities, and foibles of the single self.

In his *Phenomenology of Mind* he says that the Other Self is the only adequate mirror of my own self-conscious self; the subject can only see itself when what it sees is another self-consciousness.

What we have here is, I think, a profound and most important insight in that Hegel recognises a very significant point about self-knowledge—namely that self-knowledge cannot be achieved through mere introspection into my own (I take this to be the significance of the 'single self') feelings, foibles, habits, likes and dislikes, capacities and so on. I cannot examine the single self and reach any important conclusions because I do not exist in isolation from other selves and my introspection must of necessity be based on an examination of my relationships with others.

Hegel can be taken, at this point, to be drawing attention to the importance others play in any serious understanding and knowledge of the Self. (I am here ignoring difficulties which subsequently arise from Hegel's account of the Self and the Other. For a detailed discussion see my paper 'Hegel on the Self and the Other' in *Philosophy* Autumn 1981).

Philosophers who wish to stress the dichotomy in question do so on various grounds. Jaspers, for example, insists on the dichotomy on the grounds that there is a fundamental difference between understanding ourselves and understanding others by virtue of the fact that whenever a man thinks, he is directing his mind to something which is *not* himself.[17] Jaspers' argument, I take it, is based on the necessity of the subject's stepping out of himself, making an object of himself in order to grasp things about the object. This argument follows the model he offers of understanding others—man cannot think without an object and in thinking he is, therefore, condemned, always, to go 'outside' himself (the subject). What follows is that since we cannot step outside ourselves in order to understand ourselves as objects, in the way in which we understand others, self understanding is, in this sense, impossible; hence the dichotomy.

Jaspers' main point that whenever a man thinks, he is directing his mind to something which is *not* himself, does not contradict anything I have said so far. Neither does this statement, in itself, contradict the position which I wish to maintain—that it is through our understanding of others that we come to understand ourselves. I have insisted throughout that self *and* other understanding stems from relationships in which one stands with others. In this sense understanding the self is external to the self in that in thinking/understanding of the self, the person directs his mind to something which is not himself; he directs his mind to his actions in general as well as to actions and responses within particular relationships. Understanding oneself is, in the important sense, an owning or acceptance of one's actions *as* one's *own* actions. The acknowledgment of actions as one's own involves recognising and understanding an 'externality' which is subsequently internalised; the acknowledgment involves understanding something that is not oneself but rather something which is ascribable to oneself. Moreover, it is something which the person himself recognises and acknowledges as ascribable to himself.

One could object (on Jaspers' lines) that a dichotomy exists between self and other understanding in that where failure to understand another occurs, it is something like seeing the other as an object we are confronted with and trying to puzzle out, whereas failing to understand oneself is not and cannot be that I am confronted with an object 'I' or 'me' and trying to puzzle it out.

Now, my central argument about understanding persons revolved round the point that we cannot come to any real understanding of persons if we see them only as 'objects to be puzzled out'. Given my thesis on this issue, it is not only that the dichotomy as set up above is shown to be false but it also seems clear that the issue cannot be set up in this way—it is not the case that whereas I can see others as *objects* to be puzzled out, I cannot see myself in this way; I cannot even come to understand others *merely* as objects to be puzzled out.

It might still be thought possible to produce an argument in support of a dichotomy based on linguistic considerations. It might be pointed out that whereas it is legitimate to say (or cry in anguish) 'I don't understand him' or 'My wife does not understand me', it is not legitimate to utter such locutions regarding oneself—'I don't understand myself', some may argue, is incoherent. This difficulty can, I think, be resolved. Suppose I am having trouble making decisions or finding that objects of my desires, when attained, are turning out to be objects of my displeasure, or that my expectations of how others are going to respond to me are fairly systematically wrong. If things are going wrong in this way I might diagnose the situation as not understanding myself. In just the same way I may diagnose this very situation as not understanding the other or others involved. The difficulty which arose above about it being legitimate to say 'I don't understand him' but not legitimate to say 'I don't understand myself' can, I think, be resolved if we put the matter in terms of being ill at ease with someone and being ill at ease with oneself.

This way of putting the issue stresses the similarity of the considerations involved. In both cases the feeling of being ill at ease is the result of our lack of understanding. The result in both cases is tantamount to an inability to respond in an appropriate way because one does not understand what it is that one is supposed to respond to; one does not understand *how* to respond.

The understanding of the self *and* of others arises out of situations; the understanding is tantamount to the understanding of a situation in which one finds oneself with others. In other words, whether one is trying to understand oneself or another, the understanding in both cases develops within the context of situations one finds oneself in with others. The understanding often comes about as a result of reflection on the interaction taking place.

Again, it might be objected that whereas I can initiate a process of getting to understand other people better, I cannot initiate this in order to get to understand myself better. I can arrange to see more of a given person, see him in different situations, invite him to visit me, etc., but none of this applies to attempts to understand oneself better; thus one cannot escape the dichotomy between self and other understanding.

Now, it seems to me that this kind of argument is based on a muddle of important issues. As I said at the beginning, the question which is of crucial importance in our context is *how* it is possible to come to understand the self and others. The short answer to the objection, in the light of the argument above, is that the development of self understanding takes place within given situations and within given relationships. It is the given situation, the given relationship, which is conducive *both* to an understanding of the other and to self understanding.

Thus in initiating a process of getting to understand another better (such as arranging to see more of a given person, to see him in different situations or to invite him to one's home) the situation which is initiated may prove just as illuminating to self understanding as it may be to the understanding of the other. In such contexts one is really seeking understanding of a relationship or of an aspect of a relationship.

In trying to understand why, e.g., I find someone inhibiting, it is not just that I try to understand a fact about him or about myself; what I need to understand is a fact about the relationship existing between us. Thus I may wonder what it is about the other that I find inhibiting, that effectively stops me from reacting spontaneously, etc. In coming to understand such considerations, I come to understand the other and myself through facts about the relationship. Understanding why I am not inclined to act in certain ways towards another person is tantamount to understanding something both about myself and about him. I understand both that he is a person of a certain particular kind and that this fact has a significance for me. I understand myself in understanding the other.

This discussion also highlights the importance of publicity for the possibility of self and other understanding. The issue here hangs on what would count as mistaken understanding in our context. There is an independent check on self and other understanding which is supplied by the relationship from which such understanding stems. This is so because a person's actions, attitudes, moods and direct responses may draw attention to aspects which have been misunderstood. Such a check is ruled out in cases of mere introspection into one's own foibles, habits, likes and dislikes, capacities, what matters to one and so on. Mere introspection may supply us with an understanding of what we would wish to be like, what we aspire to; introspection may seriously mislead us about what we are really like. What we are really like manifests itself in our dealings with others within various relationships. Understanding the self and the other within a relationship and understanding facts about the relationship constitutes the only valuable (as opposed to trivial) knowledge and understanding of the self.

The importance of publicity for self understanding is also demonstrated in cases where expressing something publicly (to another person) makes one realise how one really feels, how one is affected by what is being expressed. Although this is a psychological point it has significance for self understanding. Expressing involves revealing or sharing what one feels and this in itself forces one to get clear about the feeling, view, opinion, etc., and also, often, it forces one to take a stand, to commit oneself in a certain way. Expressing an emotion intentionally may compel one to commit oneself to how far one is prepared to go, how much one is prepared to acknowledge and this, as it were, decision is in itself most revealing and aids self understanding.

Public expression provides a sharp contrast to cases where one merely introspects because, while introspecting, one might think or imagine all sorts of things about oneself and about objects of one's emotions which might prove utterly fictitious when put to the public test. The above considerations apply also in cases where the concern of others to understand one's problems serves as a condition which makes it possible for a person to gain self understanding.

An illuminating example of how the concern of another can provoke understanding of the self is given in a book by Herman Hesse. In the course of a conversation between Narziss and Goldmund, the latter says:

'. . . I no longer know myself, nor my real wishes and hopes. Once everything seemed so easy, as easy as the letters in a grammar-book: and now nothing is easy, not even those letters. I cannot tell what is to become of me, and, for now, I don't want to think about it. . . . But what trick do you use to question me thus again and again, in words that illumine my mind, and make me see into myself? . . . How

do you do it? You seem to know everything. You have taught me so
many things about our friendship which I did not understand at the
time I heard them, and later they seemed full of meaning and consequence. . . . How is it you can know me so well? Could I learn that
from you also?'[18]

In responding to the concern and interest of others, one tries to
crystallise one's problem in order to express it, thus gaining an
insight, an understanding of both what the problem one is confronted with consists in and how the given problem affects one
and why. These considerations bring in the notion of 'a matter
for concern', concern to understand and, often, concern to act as
a result. The notion of decision-making is crucial to understanding
and thus the 'concern to understand' and 'the concern to act' are
logically linked.

Coming to understand oneself through discussion of one's
problems, of emotions, or of things that matter to one is an
extremely important way of coming by understanding of the self.
Just as in cases of understanding others, self understanding which
comes about via the sharing of concerns and interests, acquires an
objectivity through being open to corrections and/or criticism
and thus the vital notion of checks on correctness and incorrectness gets a hold.

Thus, one does not come by self understanding through introspection independently of one's relationships and understanding
of others. There is, I suggest, no dichotomy between self understanding and understanding of one's relationships. Equally, there
is no dichotomy between understanding others and understanding
relationships with them. Therefore, in an important sense, there is
no dichotomy between self understanding and other understanding. Understanding oneself and understanding others consists
largely of the understanding of the various relationships; largely
in virtue of the way in which one is, or comes to be, inserted into
them. The growth of self understanding is thus not independent
of the growth of understanding of others. It is for this reason
that, it seems to me, no dichotomy is possible. At most we can
separate out different aspects of a complex phenomenon.

What I think finally emerges from the above discussion is that
self understanding involves and is based on intersubjectivity and
that any real understanding of the self cannot be achieved unless

it stems from intersubjective situations. Intersubjectivity is essential to the subjective life and understanding of the self. The subjectivity under discussion throughout this book is thus not used in the privative interpretation of this term; it is logically linked to intersubjectivity in a way analogous to that in which objectivity is linked to and is dependent on intersubjectivity. Each subject's life has a centre outside itself though it may be centred on a varied range of interests. Understanding the self is an understanding of one's central interests—be they persons, intellectual pursuits, virtues or vices. Whatever those central interests are for any given subject they are essentially outside himself and therefore, in large measure, intersubjective.

I think that I have said enough to show that there is no real separation between self and other understanding; one's own nature can only be adequately understood in terms of one's involvements with others and one's understanding of them.

I have, in this chapter, gone some way towards spelling out what sort of circumstances are necessary to the development of personal understanding and what is involved in the power to provoke such understanding on a deep level. The problem which must be answered now, following the arguments offered throughout (that deep understanding of another is only possible within personal relationships) can, perhaps, be stated as follows: How different is the understanding within personal relationships from the understanding of others in cases where no such relationship exists? This could be formulated as follows: 'What is it that you understand about x that I, who also know him, cannot understand or even in principle come to know, unless I also stand in some personal relationship to him?'

It is to the answering of this problem that I must now address myself.

Notes

1 M. Merleau-Ponty, *Phenomenology of Perception*, trans. C. Smith, Routledge & Kegan Paul, London, 1962, pp. 156ff.

2 T. Penelhum, 'Pleasure and Falsity'—Symposium. *American Philosophical Quarterly*, Vol. 1, No. 2 (April 1964), p. 83.

3 I am indebted to J. M. Cohen for the notion of emotions as spurs to actions as also for some very illuminating examples.

4 R. S. Peters, 'Emotions and the Category of Passivity', *PAS*, Vol. LXII (1961/2).

5 *Ibid.* p. 119.
6 *Ibid.* p. 117.
7 R. S. Peters, 'Reason and Passion', in *The Proper Study*, Royal Institute of Philosophy Lectures, Vol. IV, 1969/70, Macmillan, 1971.
8 *Ibid.* pp. 137-8.
9 *Ibid.* p. 138.
10 *Ibid.* p. 141.
11 *Ibid.* pp. 143-4.
12 *Ibid.* p. 151.
13 *Ibid.* p. 151.
14 *Ibid.* pp. 143-4.
15 *Ibid.* p. 147. (my italics)
16 S. I. Benn, 'Freedom, Autonomy and the Concept of Person', *PAS*, Vol. LXXVI (1975/6), p. 127.
17 K. Jaspers, *Reason and Existenz*, trans. W. Earle, New York, 1955.
18 Hermann Hesse, *Narziss and Goldmund*, trans. G. Dunlop, Penguin, 1973, p. 63.

6 *Understanding Persons Within Personal Relationships*

MY main problem, following arguments offered in the previous chapter, is twofold:

1. Given that a certain kind of deep understanding of another is only possible within a personal relationship which is rich in both its rational and emotional aspects, what is it that a person, standing in such a relationship with another, is able to understand that another person, who does not stand within a personal relationship with that other, is precluded from understanding?

2. If we cannot separate emotions and their effects from ways of seeing the world, and seeing and understanding selves and others in situations, how is it that emotions supply what I called the vital context in which one's understanding of the self and of others develops?

Since the two aspects of my problem are very closely inter-related I shall take them largely together.

I have argued that the growth of understanding within a personal relationship is not and cannot be solely intellectual; it is also strongly related to emotional growth. This needs now to be illustrated.

6.1 Emotions and Personal Relationships

Much of the understanding which we have of ourselves and of others is an understanding of the emotions and their role as springs of our actions. Understanding another's emotions and feelings is a part of understanding him. Emotions of all kinds act as an essential spur to our understanding of others. Conrad draws our attention to this point:

I suspect that he had been roughly handled by Captain Anthony up there, and the resentment gave a tremendous fillip to the slow play of his wits. Those men of sober fancy, when anything rouses their imaginative faculty, are very thorough.[1]

John Bayley also stresses the importance of emotional involvement to our understanding:

We desire in obedience to the fixed patterns of our sexual imagination, but we fall in love because we are really seeing another person. Love is the potentiality of men and women which keeps them most interested in each other, ... Nothing else that unites human beings so emphatically declares at the same time the plurality of living; . . . .[2]

Henry James says of Balzac's men and women: '. . . it was by loving them . . . that he knew them; it was not by knowing them that he loved.'[3] Again we get the expression of the importance of emotional involvement to the possibility of understanding—the stress on the priority of emotional responses which inspire growth of understanding. One's concern for understanding is intimately related to the concern for the person whom one is attempting to understand.

These sorts of considerations are inextricably bound up with human relationships in general, without the understanding of which we could not have any second level concepts of persons. To put it more strongly, we could not have an adequate understanding of the concept 'person' without having an adequate understanding of human relationships which are a part of that concept. I am, therefore, concerned particularly with the part emotions play in our understanding of others within personal relationships and how such understanding takes place. I have, for this reason, concentrated, in the previous chapter, on showing that emotions are not necessarily passive and, thus, also, not necessarily irrational in terms of the crucial role they play in our understanding.

Now, when an attempt is made to convey understanding of this kind, there is no certainty that what is being conveyed will be understood by the third person, who may be incapable of the effort of imagination required to understand; to understand not so much *what* but *how* the other feels. By this I mean the significant difference between understanding *that* the other feels a certain emotion and understanding *how* he feels—the extent and importance of the feeling, to what extent it influences his actions and view of the world. In the latter case, the effort of the imagination, however great, may fail and will fail without the support of background knowledge and understanding of the person's history, his way of expressing and describing things, his particular personality and his disposition to say, feel, do things in certain ways, an understanding which grows and develops within personal relationships. Personal relationships provide *the context* within which one is enabled to understand a person's intimate springs of action in their widest sense. When trying to verbalise something of what has been understood, one has, as it were, to think about what it is one is trying to convey and the all-important feeling one is trying to convey often eludes one (as in the Swann example). The more absorbed or involved one becomes, the more difficult it is to put such situations into words.

How one acts, what accompanies certain utterances, the tone of voice, the amount of sensed enthusiasm, what is stressed and such considerations become much more revealing within what I called the 'context'. By contrast, one tends, very often, to be somewhat suspicious of people who are very articulate about themselves, who give powerful and vivid accounts of their feelings; one wonders whether what they describe is genuinely felt. Another quotation from Conrad is apposite:

To render a crucial point of feeling in terms of human speech is really an impossible task. Written words can only form a sort of translation. And if that translation happens, from want of skill or from over-anxiety, to be too literal, the people caught in the toils of passion, instead of disclosing themselves, which would be an art, are made to give themselves away, which is neither art nor life. Nor yet truth! At any rate, not the whole truth; for it is truth robbed of all its necessary and sympathetic reservations and qualifications which give it its fair form, its just proportions, its semblance of human fellowship.[4]

An important aspect of the kind of understanding under discussion is that we assimilate and learn things from our relationships with another which could not be expressed in words or which, very often, we are not even aware of; we are made aware of new possibilities. Here again, a conscious effort renders what one is trying to convey rather elusive or, as importantly, may distort its essence. John Bayley puts this point very clearly:

It is a profound irony of the play, an irony inherent in Shakespeare's vision, that we cannot say 'Othello is a great man with feet of clay', or, 'Othello loves not Desdemona but his own idea of himself', without putting ourselves outside the world of love which the play presents.

By making such definitions we lose the world which Iago cannot understand and has never experienced. But without risking these definitions, it may be objected, how can we understand the play? The answer is, of course, that the medium of dramatic poetry has already implied them for us, for it is one of the properties of the greatest dramatic poetry to suggest complexities of character which are beyond the scope of the most exacting discursive analysis, which cover the expanse of the work like ripples on water and lose their nature if caught up in the hand.[5]

Bayley speaks in terms of an author conveying the complexities of the characters in the context of a work but I take this to be very closely analogous to cases of understanding where the context is that of personal relationships, and where equally, we cannot adequately capture all that is involved in this understanding in a convenient set of statements of the kind: 'I understand that . . .' (in Bayley's terms 'definitions'). It seems clear that we have here a very different kind of understanding which cannot be reduced to some one account in terms of necessary or sufficient conditions for what is to count as understanding in general, to sets of criteria or specific kinds of explanations. The question whether someone has understood or what it is he understands remains very difficult to answer. It can only be answered in terms of a given context which in this case is the situation of the two persons concerned. I have already discussed some of the difficulties involved here by arguing that a demand for a priori criteria is misguided in certain contexts.

An objection could be raised that what I have said comes close to contradicting my argument that there is necessarily something propositional about understanding in that the propositional nature of understanding follows from the fact that what can be understood is normally expressible in words. This objection must be met as it rests on a misunderstanding.

I said above that the kind of understanding under discussion is often not one which can be stated in terms of: 'I understand that . . .'. Our understanding here focuses on and consists in understanding a person and this involves much more than just understanding things *about* that person which can be stated in the form of 'I understand that . . .'. In addition, much of the understanding is engaged in and manifests itself in a lived situation which is the context of understanding.

This kind of understanding can also be expressed in words by describing what is going on, e.g., how and why one responded in a certain way in a given situation. What it is that has been understood falls within the complex description of the experienced situations but the *quality* of the understanding cannot often be captured in words. This quality stems from the expressiveness and significance which persons have for each other within personal relationships and these also contain an all-important emotional dimension.

Emotions, however, are not reducible to words, nor need they be; emotions provoke understanding, they are not equivalent with understanding. Thus, what it is one claims to understand, within a personal relationship, is expressible in words and therefore fulfils my condition of a necessary propositional content but the quality of this kind of understanding, which stems directly from the context in which it develops, cannot be conveyed explicitly. *How* one comes by such understanding, with all the complexities involved, cannot be adequately captured in words. Statements about what has been understood are lifted out of the all-important context within which the understanding developed and for this reason a certain amount of distortion is inescapable. This is what I mean by saying that we cannot capture all that is involved in the understanding in a convenient set of statements; we capture the bare bones stripped of much of the quality which clothes them. Bayley's point stresses analogous difficulties in literature. Words are the tools of the writer; to be articulate about the expressiveness and significance which persons have for each other in lived situations is, at times, an intolerable struggle. As T. S. Eliot puts it so vividly in *The Four Quartets* (Burnt Norton V, L. 149):

> Words strain,
> Crack and sometimes break, under the burden,
> Under the tension, slip, slide, perish,
> Decay with imprecision, will not stay in place,
> Will not stay still.

The notion of context is vital and cannot be separated from understanding. Let us consider the example of a man in love—such a man has to be understood in the context of this love. His love is bound to influence his other activities and relationships. It may be decisive for what sort of other attachments he is prepared to form, the way he acts towards others, what other things he gets involved in and, perhaps, most importantly, it may greatly influence how he views the world; a view which may have altered radically in respect of the sort of attitudes he held previously. His relationship is now a vital part of his situation, the context within which he is to be understood.

One's emotions, whatever they are, carry with them most important ramifications for other aspects of one's life. Our understanding of others and of ourselves depends on our understanding of this crucial connection. Real understanding involves understanding of the person's emotional life—how this affects him as a subject—his wants, desires, what really matters to him and why.

These aspects manifest themselves within a relationship and mutual responses act as a vital check in terms of the appropriateness or inappropriateness of responses and thus on what has been understood. The understanding two people have of each other within personal relationships finds expression in behaviour, in responses, in interactions and develops through such responses and interactions.

In order to show what this kind of understanding amounts to, what it 'concretely' consists in, illustrations from literature are, I think, rather helpful. Examples can be used to convey what is involved in the deep understanding two people have of each other within a personal relationship, as the crucial context within which such understanding develops and manifests itself is to a large extent supplied for us. What one is trying to understand here is the expressiveness people have for each other which literature also can manifest. By using these examples I hope to show, in detail, both what personal understanding consists in and how it is that emotions supply the vital context in which one's understanding develops.

6.2 Introduction to Examples of Person Understanding within Personal Relationships

Before attempting to give and discuss such examples, there are two points which need particularly to be cleared up:

1. I may have given the impression that I lay great store by what

is usually termed 'intuitive knowledge'. I do not think that I am particularly concerned with intuitive knowledge as such, whatever that may be.

To know or to understand something we may know or understand it explicitly or implicitly. If we claim to know or understand something explicitly this entails our being able to formulate this knowledge or understanding in words, propositions, or statements or our being able to give the sort of explanations which will serve to justify our claim. Conversely, implicit knowledge or understanding cannot be stated, often cannot be verbalised and has, therefore, to be shown as implicit in, say, a description of a given situation.

Now, this, I think, differs radically from what is usually taken as intuitive knowledge precisely in respect of the latter's being statable but not justifiable. Whatever else intuitive knowledge involves, its main feature is a claim of the form 'I just know that x'. Examples of this are the wife who 'just knows' that her husband is unfaithful to her—she cannot offer a description of their situation or anything else that would serve to show some basis for this knowledge. There is nothing like this involved in this case; she just knows. Similarly, the Rocking Horse winner in D. H. Lawrence's short story, who constantly predicts the winners of horse races simply by riding a rocking horse, has no justification or explanation to offer for his knowledge—he just knows which horse will win.

It seems to me that whatever intuitive knowledge may be, its essence is that it rules out any possibility of a rationale and this is its defining criterion; once a rationale, however nebulous, is given, such knowledge ceases to count as intuitive. Intuitive knowledge amounts to either knowing how to do something without knowing what this knowledge consists in or, alternatively, it is knowledge of something statable in the form 'I know that x'. It is essentially knowledge which lacks any basis—one *just* knows. Consequently, when such knowledge is demonstrated by a skill or expressed in propositional form, nothing further can be said in support.

The kind of knowledge and understanding I am concerned with involves much more than this and, often, as I said above, is not of the form 'I know/understand that x'. There is a basis, arising from the personal relationships within which personal understanding develops, a complex context within which the understanding manifests itself and from which it stems. Expressing what such understanding consists in, very often, cannot be captured in convenient sets of propositions but it can be shown to some greater or lesser extent *as* based on, or implicit in, the object of understanding. I mean that if it is necessary to express one's understanding this can be done by one's description of a situation within which the understanding arose. The description of the situation provides the basis or the rationale of the understanding even though, often, what it is precisely that has been understood cannot be stated in the form 'I understand that x'. In other words, implicit in one's description of a situation is the understanding one has of it. It is shown in the description though not stated. This does not rule out the possibility that intuitive knowledge is also involved; I only wish to stress that the personal understanding under discussion is not primarily of an intuitive kind for the reasons given.

2. Since I am about to make extensive use of examples from literature to illustrate what the kind of understanding I am concerned with involves, a few remarks are necessary to clarify my position regarding such examples. There is a limit to what one can usefully expect here; I do not think that literature can teach us to feel an emotion.

However vivid a description of the feelings of, say, a man facing death may be, we cannot learn from such a description what *the* feeling, which accompanies the waiting for death, is. (This example is taken from J. Benson's 'Emotion and Expression'.[6]) We cannot learn this from a description for at least two important reasons. Firstly, the postulated possibility of learning to feel such an emotion implies that there is an emotion x of a type felt by all condemned men. This, it seems to me, just is not the case for the various reasons given in the previous chapter. Secondly, such a particular emotion is outside our experience as also is the character in the novel and this brings in all the difficulties which I discussed in relation to empathy.

As Benson says, sometimes a novel may make us think that we have been given some understanding of the emotion which is outside our experience. But, it seems, this is different from having learned to feel the emotion. One can come to learn to feel an emotion but this inevitably involves experience. I will not go into what might be involved in learning to feel an emotion except to mention that the crucial factor here is the coming to feel an emotion through an experience of a personal nature. This is not to say, however, that we cannot come to understand much of what a given experience means to the character in question which is different from learning to feel the emotion itself. Our understanding may be deepened but it cannot come into real being for us just from a description if it is outside our experience.

Literature can teach us something about a man's condition, the shape and motives of human conduct, by providing the context emotional and material, for self-knowledge and an awareness of others. It deals essentially and continually with the image of man, it mirrors what has often been described as 'the human condition'. The novel has its most powerful appeal when it makes connections with something already familiar to us in our experience. The understanding which it manifests is more accessible to our grasp.

But literature also, importantly, teaches us to discriminate, to question, and thus acts as a challenge to our personal prejudices and misconceptions. A quotation from Solzhenitsyn captures the issue:

But who will reconcile these scales of values (of different nations) and how? Who will create for mankind a single system of valuation—for evil deeds and good deeds, for what is intolerable and what is tolerable, for how the line is to be drawn between them today? Who will explain to mankind what is really terrible and unbearable, and what only irritates our skin because it is near? Who will direct our anger against that which is truly terrible and not that which is merely near? Who could carry the understanding of this through the barrier of his own human experience? Who would be able to bring home to a bigoted and obstinate human being the distant grief and joy of other people, the understanding of relationships and misconceptions that he himself has never experienced? Propaganda, compulsion and scientific proof are all powerless here . . . the means to convey all this to us does exist in the world. It is Art. It is literature. Art and literature can perform the miracle of overcoming man's characteristic weakness of learning only by his own experience, so that experience of others passes him by.[7]

This passage highlights the difficulties I have discussed. Writers can create the context for us in which superficial understanding can be transformed from the abstract to a personal level. Reporting events in other parts of the world does not really touch our understanding. This distinction is also made by Conrad:

Information is something one goes out to seek and puts away when found as you might a piece of lead; ponderous, useful, unvibrating, dull. Whereas knowledge comes to one, this sort of knowledge, a chance acquisition preserving in its repose a fine resonant quality.[8]

Solzhenitsyn's own works are most powerful examples of this challenge to think and learn to discriminate in terms of experiences of others. A single book which does this by presenting us with different aspects of something momentous is Tolstoy's *War and Peace*. The young Rostov and his friends sweep us into their lives where war is romantic; its stark tragedy is outweighed by the excitement and glamour of living dangerously, joyously and to the limit. But we also come to see the moral judgment of the author in his use of Pierre's eye sweeping the battlefield of Borodino. Detached, yet compassionate, Pierre's remorseless eye, which sees more than the landscape confronting him, has the impersonality, detachment and stark vividness of a television camera focusing on horrors in our time. This is not inconsistent with an involvement with the surface romance of war, but we are enabled to contain within it a sense of moral perspective and through Pierre we are shown, we sense, the carnage and futility. We see the giant—Napoleon—in perspective; we see him as one more manipulator of men who failed because ambition overcame his sense of humanity.

When Sartre says that art is the ability 'to create something that has the capacity to touch other human beings',[9] he is reiterating what all great artists, including Solzhenitsyn, say—art is 'feeling'. For Sartre this feeling is in the intangible 'presence' behind great works of art which give life its meaning; without this presence there would be nothingness and in nothingness there is no meaning. The essence of art is imagination; for Sartre this is an 'infective' quality, it is this 'intangible presence' which conveys understanding. The words 'infection', 'activity', 'reciprocity' suggest the organic nature of literature; it does not exist in isolation, it is a means of a connection with life. In real life our view of persons and situations is often partial, hampered by compromise, vested interests, a lack of interest or an unwillingness to get involved but, as importantly, our understanding is partial because of our inability to make fine discriminations. We are bound by circumstances and the personalities involved. Through literature it is possible to become involved in and reflect on many different situations, to discuss with others, who are in the same position as ourselves, as spectators. It is often far easier to become 'involved' with characters in literature because such an involvement does not in any way compromise us: 'After all it is only a book'.

The mode of response made by a reader to a novel can be regarded as an extension of the mode of response made by on-lookers to actual events. The reader can achieve a response of involvement and reciprocity through insights into the lives of other persons who, although they live in the world of fiction, have been created by the living author who has things to say about people in the real world.

Admittedly, literature provides us only with the possibility of an imaginative sharing of participants' experiences as opposed to imaginatively sharing experiences of live persons with whom one stands in personal relationships. But the important aspects of this imaginative sharing are the reader's attempts at evaluating fictional characters and understanding what they do, what they enjoy and what they suffer. Such an evaluation begins with the reader's imaginative involvement leading to his judgment on conflicts and their resolutions, and finally reaches beyond the story to an examination of how the author is using it to propose an evaluation of possible human experience.

It could be said that by its very nature literature has a special and crucial role in illuminating our understanding and refining our powers of discrimination. Literature, licensed by its fictionality, is capable of extending and, in a sense, realising a human capacity for experience that goes beyond the limitations of any one life. It is not that literature can teach us what to do, but by actively engaging our imagination it can extend our response to life, extend our powers of judgment; through the subject matter of literature one finds demands made on the reader in which his emotions can be refined and enriched. Literature of necessity deals with human beings, their conduct, their emotions and their relationships; by its handling of this subject matter it gives expression to, and so communicates, to the reader. We can learn to be impartial in the sense that we can recognise what is at stake when being egoistical, we can also learn to be fully aware of what it is to be honest. This is what Sartre largely means by the 'infective' quality. Through an effort of the imagination the reader can fulfil the demands of literature which enables his emotions to become refined and his understanding enriched.

The writer of good literature, Tolstoy maintains, is able to render meaning more clearly, accessibly and strongly than others could.[10] The manifestation of understanding in the novel stems from a description of personal relationships in their rich contexts of interaction of persons in situations. Examples from literature render accessible the deep understanding which is inaccessible outside personal relationships.

To make claims, as I have done, that literature can help with our understanding is not to make good a much stronger claim, which has been made by, e.g., Leavis and others, that responsive reading of literature effects changes in us. To support this strong claim it would be necessary to show either that there is empirical evidence that people who read responsively are capable of greater understanding of others or that they become morally better human beings. This, it would seem, can only mean that they can deal more successfully with personal relationships, lead better lives, etc. I do not see how one could establish the necessary criteria in this context.

Nevertheless, to read Blake, Aeschylus, Shakespeare or Dante is to make a voyage of discovery of insights, knowledge, perspective; to feel not that we have participated in life as it is but that we have glimpsed what it might be. Ultimately literature can only be understood through experience. It demands Yeats' 'self-knowledge' or Newman's 'wide receptivity'. That is why my claim is more modest—I only suggest that literature may help understanding and thereby *may* affect changes in us. Whether it will do so or not depends on our personal limitations of response in the same way in which it limits us in our understanding of persons. Literature tries to provide conditions which surround situations as similar as possible to those present within personal relationships. Literature is a giant conversation on which we are privileged to eavesdrop, to enjoy other people's feelings, to perceive and understand the nature and infinite variety of human relationships. What we learn from it and how much we learn depends on our own personal limitations of understanding and response. There always remains the difficulty to what extent a reader can overcome what Solzhenitsyn calls 'man's characteristic weakness' of learning only by his own experience.

6.3 Examples of Understanding Persons within Personal Relationships

To begin with, let us take examples from *Middlemarch*.[11] Dorothea is a character who wants to do great things in the world and in an important way is most emphatically not a feminist. She has a set of principles which she tries to live up to: to develop to the full her natural feminine capacity for devotion and submissiveness. In the first chapter she thinks: 'The really delightful marriage must be that where your husband was a sort of father, and could teach you even Hebrew, if you wished it.'[12] Her complete lack of feminine frivolity, her need for spiritual sacrifice are facts of her character which prepare us admirably for what is to come. On meeting Casaubon, Dorothea decides that she has met the right man for her. She does not see him so much as a husband but as the ideal man, and as a result her feelings for him are predominantly those of daughter to father. Casaubon finds that he is incapable of real love for anyone. Dorothea is completely self-deceived about the importance of her personal desires vis-à-vis her principles which she has decided upon as most suitable for a worthwhile life. An example of this is her trying to explain to herself that she is not really bitterly disappointed at Casaubon's insistence that she take a companion on their honeymoon so that he can 'feel more at liberty' to pursue his research. She tries to subdue her annoyance: ' "Surely I am in a strangely selfish weak state of mind", she said to herself. "How can I have a husband who is so much above me without knowing that he needs me less than I need him?" '[13]

This passage shows her determination to remain convinced that she has done the right and noble thing in marrying Casaubon. Casaubon is revealed to the reader as one of Eliot's most interesting characters. He behaves and sees the world as solely scholarly. He is incapable of imagination and feeling, the kind of feeling which is essential to understanding something of people different from himself. Thus his courtship of Dorothea is not one which arises from his feelings for her but one which he constructs out of his literary memory of what courtship ought to be. This is not deliberate on his part, he just cannot do otherwise:

He determined to abandon himself to the stream of feeling, and perhaps was surprised to find what an exceedingly shallow rill it was . . . he concluded that the poets had much exaggerated the force of masculine passion.[14]

Casaubon wants very much to do the right thing but does not know how. He also begins to realise his failure as a scholar. A passage which follows here is most revealing: 'She was as blind to his inward troubles as he to hers'. We have here a relationship which is in a significant way impersonal; it lacks any real feeling. Both see each other as objects but not as objects of real emotions in that we come to understand that they are impersonal objects to each other. When Casaubon questions his lack of feeling, his answer takes the form of an assurance that it is not Dorothea's fault as he cannot think of any other woman who would please him better. Dorothea, we feel, would also be just as happy with any other scholarly person, perhaps happier. Dorothea's chief attraction to Casaubon amounts to her capacity to believe in him and worship him or rather his intellect. When Ladislaw enters into the situation Casaubon feels threatened in this respect, he fears that Ladislaw may get Dorothea to see him as he really is. Eliot describes this as a strange kind of jealousy:

There is a sort of jealousy which needs very little fire: it is hardly a passion, but a blight bred in the cloudy, damp despondency of uneasy egoism.[15]

But, however egoistic the jealousy, he really feels for the first time and this enables him to sharpen his awareness. His feeling himself threatened forces an insight into Dorothea's thoughts which he was previously incapable of:

. . . there had entered into the husband's mind a certainty that she judged him, and that her wifely devotedness was like a penitential expiation of unbelieving thoughts— . . . .[16]

But it is important to see that his understanding of Dorothea is limited to his understanding of her thoughts; he is still incapable of understanding her feelings. His jealousy has nothing to do with the possibility of a relationship developing between Dorothea and Ladislaw; on the contrary, the possibility that they are or will become lovers does not even occur to him.

Dorothea finally comes to understand Casaubon as a person when she is moved by pity towards him during his illness. She very gradually begins to see him as he really is and her pity grows to profound compassion for him which makes her realise that she has to give the promise he demands of her (to complete his work after his death):

Neither law nor the world's opinion compelled her to this—only her husband's nature and her own compassion, only the ideal, and not the real yoke of marriage. She saw clearly enough the whole situation, yet she was fettered and she could not smite the stricken soul that entreated hers.[17]

It is not until Dorothea is able to feel a personal emotion towards Casaubon that she begins to achieve an understanding which is personal, in complete contrast to the impersonal understanding of him as an object—a suitable object for a husband. It is not until disillusion with her ideas and principles sets in, not until she gives up her fight to sustain her self-deception that she becomes aware of Casaubon as a person in his own right—a real person not an imaginary object of intellect worthy of her devotion. It is not until she feels deep pity for him that she is finally capable of a genuine act of devotion, involving genuine sacrifice, when she is ready to give her promise entirely for his sake. The contrast in or change in her understanding can best be illustrated by the relevant quotations:

We are all of us born in moral stupidity, taking the world as an udder to feed our supreme selves: Dorothea had clearly begun to emerge from that stupidity, but yet it had been easier to her to imagine how she would devote herself to Mr. Casaubon, and become wise and strong in his strength and wisdom, than to conceive with that distinctness which is no longer reflection but feeling—an idea wrought back to the directness of sense, like the solidity of objects—that he had an equivalent centre of self, whence the light and the shadows must always fall with a certain difference.[18]

When the change comes it results in a qualitative change of her understanding:

She was no longer struggling against the perception of facts, but adjusting herself to their clearest perception; and now when she looked steadily at her husband's failure, still more at his possible consciousness of failure, she seemed to be looking along the one track where duty became tenderness.[19]

Now Dorothea is able to realise that her understanding of Casaubon must not be merely intellectual but must go through a crucible of feeling before she can form a proper relationship with him, not as a strong man and a scholar, but as a *person*, weaker than herself. She is now able to see their life together with a new insight, from a different point of view and the situations of life take on a new meaning.

One of the most revealing examples of personal understanding is to be found in *The Wings of the Dove*.[20] Henry James deals masterfully with insights into various relationships. He sets up no moral values *as a whole* in his novels. He strives to see each person's viewpoint on relationships through that person's eyes, so that the reader is left with a sense of the complicated nature of relationships. The reader feels the potentiality for the translucency of experience of the characters in relationships, but also their limitations because they can only see it all through their eyes. At the end the author has made no judgment but he has made the reader see the character's viewpoints, why they have behaved in certain ways due to their limited vision.

James traces for us the process of one character coming to a deep understanding of another in such a way as to make the reader see that it isn't always the full truth. The reader sees each character responding to the other in terms of his/her own values, his/her limitations. The characters reflect on their actions within their relationships emotionally and therefore, often, with great pain, and intellectually and therefore with a certain detachment which enables them to come to positive resolutions with some honesty.

We have here two illuminating strands of complex under-standing: one is the understanding Mrs. Stringham, Milly's travelling companion, has of Milly, an understanding which develops as their close personal relationship develops; the other is the understanding which Densher painfully comes to achieve. The important aspects of the novel can best be shown by quoting from the introduction by Herbert Read:

The motive was one which James had for a long time nursed in his imagination. 'The idea, reduced to its essence, is that of a young person conscious of a great capacity for life, but early stricken and doomed, condemned to die under short respite, while also enamoured of the world; aware moreover of the condemnation and passionately desiring to "put in" before extinction as many of the finer vibrations as possible, and so achieve, however briefly and brokenly, the sense of having lived'. . . . The author plunges her, eager and disingenuous, into a corner of English society which might be described as a little gamy—at least, it mingles its finer feelings with speculations which are calculating, even in the crude sense. Kate Croy, who threatens to dominate the novel by the forcefulness of her character, is more than a foil to Milly's wistful innocence; she represents the moral ambiguity of a diplomatic approach to life—which is the typical Jamesian theme, not less important for being so seemingly subtle. Her emissary, who is also her lover, is a weaker figure: indeed, we can never quite believe in Merton Densher, so deeply is his masculinity compromised in this petticoat government. The plot which these two concoct is staged in Venice, in an atmosphere of watery corruption which James knew as no one else how to convey. Kate instigates a particularly foul piece of deception—foul because, however extenuating the circumstances, it did involve the sanctity of the passions: the passion which was hers and Densher's by natural development, and poor Milly's only on the basis of their unconscionable pretence.

A moral tragedy cannot be epitomised: its excitement is in its subtleties of observation, its accuracy of discrimination, its accumu-lated perception of issues and dilemmas; and above all in the author's conscious control of the final issue. It might be objected that in this tragedy the heroine is not a victim claimed by exacting gods: she dies full of pity and forgiveness, and the retribution is left to work its poison in the consciences of the calculating lovers.

Mrs. Stringham loves Milly with a love which is protective and admiring but, most importantly, with a love that allows Milly to be utterly herself:

Mrs. Stringham by this time understood everything, was more than ever confirmed in wonder and admiration, in her view that it was life enough simply to feel her companion's feelings; but there were special keys she had not yet added to her bunch, impressions that, of a sudden, were apt to affect her as new. . . .

At the end of a week, however, with their further progress, her young friend had effectively answered the question (why she was so restless) and given her the impression, indistinct indeed as yet, of something that had a reality compared with which the nervous explanation would have been coarse. Mrs. Stringham found herself from that hour, in other words, in presence of an explanation that remained a muffled and intangible form, but that, assuredly, should it take on sharpness, would explain everything and more than everything, would become instantly the light in which Milly was to be read.

Such a matter as this may at all events speak of the style in which our young woman could affect those who were near her, may testify to the sort of interest she could inspire. She worked—and seemingly quite without design—upon the sympathy, the curiosity, the fancy of her associates, and we shall really ourselves scarce otherwise come closer to her than by feeling their impression and sharing, if need be, their confusion.[21]

During one of their walks in the mountains Milly moves away from Mrs. Stringham and is later discovered by her sitting on a slab of rock overhanging a precipice. The image of the girl remained with Mrs. Stringham and took on the character of a revelation:

During the breathless minutes of her watch she had seen her companion afresh; the latter's type, aspect, marks, her history, her state, her beauty, her mystery, all unconsciously betrayed themselves to the Alpine air, and all had been gathered in again to feed Mrs. Stringham's flame.[22]

Mrs. Stringham realises early on, following her insight into Milly's character, that their relationship is to be profoundly more complex than expected. Her commitment to Milly enables her to sense and understand things to an astonishing degree. James stresses in the above passage the delicacy of human relationships.

When Milly is introduced to Kate and Densher we are given a contrast—Kate, although fond of Milly, is always ready to understand so much and no more than she finds convenient for her purposes. Thus when Milly assures her that her illness is not serious, Kate is more than ready to accept this at its face value. Later, however, she accepts with equal ease the fact that Milly is fatally ill—this suits her purposes admirably as she can now put her plan into operation. Accordingly, she persuades Densher to court Milly and marry her thus enabling him to inherit Milly's money, money which is essential to their own marriage. Densher, after some qualms, agrees to the scheme, motivated by his love for Kate. He does not really see, he is unable to understand the utterly distasteful implications of what he is doing, all he feels is some uneasiness; he sees no harm in lying to Milly about his feelings for Kate. Kate, who lacks real personal involvement with Milly, reveals her lack of understanding and does not realise that thereby she betrays her attitude:

'You're right about her not being easy to know. One sees her more than one sees almost anyone; but then one discovers that that isn't knowing her and that one may know better a person whom one doesn't "see", as I say, half as well.'[23]

The implication here is that we do not necessarily understand someone better by knowing more about them, by observing their presence. Mrs. Stringham who found Kate's discrimination interesting was also filled with anxiety—she looked at Kate and Densher—

. . . looked very much as some spectator in an old-time circus might have watched the oddity of a Christian maiden, in the arena, mildly, caressingly, martyred. It was the nosing and fumbling not of lions and tigers but of domestic animals let loose as for a joke.[24]

Mrs. Stringham is now able to understand that her wish for Milly's happiness with Densher is fraught with unpleasant undertones. What these are she is not yet aware of but she understands enough to put her on her guard, to see the need for protecting Milly. She begins to sense something of Densher's attitude which James reveals in the following passage:

He was on his feet by this time, to take leave (of Milly) and also because he was at last too restless. The speech in question, at least, wasn't disloyal to Kate; that was the very tone of their bargain. So was

it, by being loyal, another kind of lie, the lie of the uncandid profession of a motive. He was staying so little 'for' Milly that he was
staying positively against her. He didn't, none the less, know, and at
last, thank goodness, he didn't care.[25]

He does not realise fully what he is doing, not until his confrontation with Mrs. Stringham. He is able to be sincerely shocked
at the fact that Lord Mark has proposed to Milly. When informed
of this he is able to say:

'Hasn't he known her, into the bargain,' the young man asked—'didn't
he, weeks before, see her, judge her, feel her, as having, for such a
suit as his, not more perhaps than a few months to live?'
Mrs. Stringham at first, for reply, but looked at him in silence; and
it gave more force to what she then remarkably added. 'He has doubt-
less been aware of what you speak of, just as you have yourself been
aware.'
'He has wanted her, you mean, just *because*—?'
'Just because,' said Susan Shepherd.
'The hound!' Merton Densher brought out. He moved off, however,
with a hot face, as soon as he had spoken, conscious again of an
intention in his visitor's reserve.[26]

From the moment in which he realises that Mrs. Stringham has
understood his motives towards Milly, he begins to understand
his own actions, to see them in their proper light. He is thus able
to tell Kate:

'She must die, my dear, in her own extraordinary way.'
'Naturally. But I don't see then what proof you have that she was
ever alienated.'
'I have the proof that she refused for days and days to see me.'
'But she was ill.'
'That hadn't prevented her—as you yourself a moment ago said—
during the previous time. If it had been only illness it would have
made no difference with her.'
'She would still have received you?'
'She would still have received me.'
'Oh, well,' said Kate, 'if you know—!'
'Of course I know. I know moreover, as well, from Mrs. Stringham.'
'And what does Mrs. Stringham know?'
'Everything'. . . .

'Because you've told her?'

'Because she has seen for herself. I've told her nothing. She's a person who does see.'[27]

His realisation that Milly also understood his scheme leads him to an understanding of himself, of what he was capable of; an understanding which changes his attitude completely. He cannot now take the money Milly left him in her will. He is still willing to marry Kate, an act which would wholly reveal the futility of the revolting scheme he tried to succeed in. Kate, however, feels now that something has gone wrong with their relationship; he sees it now in a different light as a result of his deeper understanding. She questions him:

'Your word of honour that you're not in love with her memory.'

'Oh—her memory!'

'Ah'—she made a high gesture—'don't speak of it as if you couldn't be. *I* could, in your place; and you're one for whom it will do. Her memory's your love. You *want* no other.'

He heard her out in stillness, watching her face, but not moving. Then he only said: 'I'll marry you, mind you, in an hour.'

'As we were?'

'As we were.'

But she turned to the door, and her headshake was now the end. 'We shall never be again as we were!'[28]

The realisation of having lived on an illusionary plane, of the shallow level of their relationships which were considered self-sufficient, of the all-absorbing social, hollow intercourse, floods over Densher and overwhelms him. He now understands that he has made no real contact with Milly as a person, and consequently was unable to understand what she has faced up to. His guilty acknowledgment of 'conscious fools paradise' now disgusts him. He realises how much more there is to a relationship than its social aspect; in his dealings with Milly he had excluded 'life'— her pain, fear and death. Densher's insight into the greatness of her character is connected with his realisation that she faced up to these alone. Now, like Mrs. Stringham, he has come up against Milly's inner strength but, unlike her, he has already abused it. His guilt completely changes his attitudes and his own life; his future with Kate is now impossible. The important point is not that Densher has developed a conscience but that his insight and new understanding gave rise to devastating consequences arising also from his profound understanding of himself. The most diffi-cult thing for Densher to bear is that he is now helpless to put things right while Milly's generosity, compassion and forgiveness, in the light of his real understanding of her, can still reach him after her death.

The Wings of the Dove is rich in subtle descriptions of personal relationships in which understanding manifests itself. To see fully how the understanding develops and what it amounts to, it is necessary to take into account the accumulative perceptions of all the subtle issues, and this it is impossible for me to do here. My aim was to convey the necessity of real personal relationships within which this kind of personal understanding and the under-standing of self develops; to stress what is involved in the transi-tion from an impersonal to a personal understanding which re-quires a complex context and cannot be captured adequately in any clearly statable form, i.e., simply in a number of statements. We cannot shorten or simplify what is involved without losing much that is of vital significance.

My choice of examples, so far, has involved relationships built on compassion, affection and love. I do not wish to imply that it is only emotions of this kind which enable our understanding to develop. A feeling of something shared, the emotion of fear, hate or envy may have the same sort of effect.

E. M. Forster describes a situation in which a shared incident leads to the development of a very close personal relationship; mutual understanding is provoked by the incident.[29]

A young woman, Lucy, on holiday in Florence, is shopping for some photographs in the piazza. Strolling along, admiring the architecture, she is startled by a quarrel suddenly breaking out between two Italians which results in one of them being stabbed. The shock makes her faint. George Emerson, a fellow guest at the pension, appears on the scene and insists on taking her home. He retrieves the photographs which she had dropped and while walk-ing along the banks of the Arno he throws them into the river.

'Where are the photographs?'
He was silent.
'I believe it was my photographs that you threw away.'

'I didn't know what to do with them,' he cried, and his voice was that of an anxious boy. Her heart warmed towards him for the first time.

'They were covered with blood. There! I'm glad I've told you; and all the time we were making conversation I was wondering what to do with them.' He pointed downstream. 'They've gone.' The river swirled under the bridge. 'I did mind them so, and one is so foolish, it seemed better that they should go out to sea—I don't know; I may just mean that they frightened me.' Then the boy verged into a man. 'For something tremendous has happened; I must face it without getting muddled. It isn't exactly that a man has died.'

Something warned Lucy that she must stop him.

'It has happened,' he repeated, 'and I mean to find out what it is.'

'Mr. Emerson—'

He turned towards her frowning, as if she had disturbed him in some abstract quest.

'I want to ask you something before we go in.'

They were close to their pension. She stopped and leant her elbows against the parapet of the embankment. He did likewise. There is at times a magic in identity of position; it is one of the things that have suggested to us eternal comradeship. She moved her elbows before saying:

'I have behaved ridiculously.'

He was following his own thoughts.

'I was never so much ashamed of myself in my life; I cannot think what came over me.'

'I nearly fainted myself,' he said; but she felt that her attitude repelled him.

'Well, I owe you a thousand apologies.'

'Oh, all right.'

'And—this is the real point—you know how silly people are gossiping—ladies especially, I am afraid—you understand what I mean?'

'I'm afraid I don't.'

'I mean, would you not mention it to anyone, my foolish behaviour?'

'Your behaviour? Oh yes, all right—all right.'

'Thank you so much. And would you—'

She could not carry her request any further. The river was gushing below them, almost black in the advancing night. He had thrown her photographs into it, and then he had told her the reason. It struck her that it was hopeless to look for chivalry in such a man. He would do her no harm by idle gossip; he was trustworthy, intelligent, and even kind; he might even have a high opinion of her. But he lacked chivalry; his thoughts, like his behaviour, would not be modified by awe. It was useless to say to him, 'And would you—' and hope that he would

complete the sentence for himself, averting his eyes from her naked-
ness like the knight in that beautiful picture. She had been in his arms,
and he remembered it, just as he remembered the blood on the photographs that she had bought in Alinari's shop. It was not exactly that
a man had died; something had happened to the living: they had
come to a situation where character tells, and where Childhood enters
upon the branching paths of Youth.

'Well, thank you so much', she repeated. 'How quickly these accidents do happen, and then one returns to the old life!'

'I don't.'

Anxiety moved her to question him.

His answer was puzzling: 'I shall probably want to live.'

'But why, Mr. Emerson? What do you mean?'

'I shall want to live, I say.'

Leaning her elbows on the parapet, she contemplated the River
Arno, whose roar was suggesting some unexpected melody to her
ears.[30]

Her new found relationship with George sharpens her awareness to a degree which is a source of surprise to her:

Of the many things Lucy was noticing today, not the least remarkable
was this: the ghoulish fashion in which respectable people will nibble
after blood. George Emerson had kept the subject strangely pure.[31]

Their sudden shared experience of death and, on another occasion,
a profound shared experience of beauty, gives them the magic
'identity of position' which transmits them from the separating
level of social intercourse so that, for a moment, there is real
contact between them which, we see later, Lucy, despite efforts
to the contrary, realises that she cannot deny. Years later, she
meets George again but is by this time engaged to another man
and determined to do the 'right thing'. She finds, however, that
she cannot go through with her marriage and decides, therefore,
to go on a long journey. On the eve of her departure she accident-
ally meets George's father in a friend's house and a long conversation between them develops in which he tries to save her
from what he calls 'the muddle'. He shows her that life's 'muddles', missed opportunities and misguided loyalties are life's
greatest dangers, as is self-deception and thus the denial of one's
own true feelings:

G

'Take an old man's word: there's nothing worse than a muddle in all
the world. It is easy to face Death and Fate, and the things that sound
so dreadful. It is on my muddles that I look back with horror—on the
things that I might have avoided. We can help one another but little.
I used to think I could teach young people the whole of life, but I
know better now, and all my teaching of George has come down to
this: beware of muddle. . . . Do you remember before, when you
refused the room with the view? Those were muddles—little, but
ominous—and I am fearing that you are in one now. . . . You love
George!' And after his long preamble, the three words burst against
Lucy like waves from the open sea. . . . She summoned physical
disgust. 'You're shocked, but I mean to shock you. It's the only hope
at times. I can reach you no other way. . . . I have no time for the
tenderness, and the comradeship, and the poetry, and the things that
really matter, ... Truth counts, Truth does count.' . . . .

He gave her a sense of deities reconciled, a feeling that, in gaining
the man she loved, she would gain something for the whole world.
Throughout the squalor of her homeward drive—she spoke at once—
his salutation remained. He had robbed the body of its taint, the
world's taunts of their sting; he had shown her the holiness of direct
desire. She 'never exactly understood', she would say in after years,
'how he managed to strengthen her. It was as if he had made her see
the whole of everything at once.'[32]

Lucy is much moved by this incident. She realises that she came
to understand something of great importance, something that
profoundly changed her life. In a vital way the incident shocked
her into an understanding of herself but she cannot herself
verbalise what it is she had come to understand. She can only do
so up to a point, she can only describe the profundity of that
understanding as: 'It was as if he had made her see the whole of
everything at once'. We have here an example of a person standing
in close personal relationship both to his son and to Lucy. He is
able to make Lucy see, to shock Lucy into coming to understand
herself, to understand her own feelings and to free her of her
self-deception. Although he is shown in the novel as a bystander
in the sense that he rarely talks to Lucy, this, nevertheless, does
not preclude him from forming a personal relationship with her.
His relationship with his son is a mutual personal relationship but
that with Lucy is very much one-sided. Lucy, up to the point of
their dramatic encounter, has only a most superficial understanding of him—he is seen mainly as George's father. In shocking her

into self-understanding, he also enables her to see him, for the first time, as the person he really is, what he has become as a result of great suffering. He gives her courage to face the consequences of her 'muddle', courage which arises directly from her understanding of him in the context of his past life history.

Finally, I want to turn to *Othello*, where we are given an example of understanding based on hatred. Iago states his hatred and the reasons which inspired it at the beginning of the play, in his first speech. He also makes quite clear his overwhelming wish for revenge:

> 'In following him, I follow but myself.
> Heaven is my judge, not I for love and duty,
> But seeming so, for my peculiar end;
> For when my outward action does demonstrate
> The native act, and figure of my heart,
> In complement extern, 'tis not long after
> But I will wear my heart upon my sleeve
> For doves to peck at: I am not what I am.'[33]

Shakespeare builds up a vivid picture of Iago, such that his actions are a progression of steps in the development of his thinking, most revealing of the man himself. At first Iago is bent merely on making mischief but soon finds that Othello's prestige and qualities of character can overcome slanders which Iago tries to perpetrate. He now realises that the attack must be more direct, he must work on Othello himself; Iago's understanding becomes, accordingly, more acute. Thus, when Othello is confronted by Desdemona's irate father, Iago is there to learn what he can from the situation. After Othello's passionate declaration of love for Desdemona, when Brabantio says:

> 'Look to her, Moor, have a quick eye to see:
> She has deceiv'd her father, may do thee.'[34]

Iago remembers the words and although at the moment he does not realise their full significance and power, the time comes when he sees them as the potentially deadly weapon against Othello's weakest spot.

Iago now makes a conscious effort at understanding Othello.

He knows that this is the only way in which he can be effective in devising means to his destruction:

> 'The Moor a free and open nature too,
> That thinks men honest that but seem to be so:
> And will as tenderly be led by the nose
> As asses are.
> I ha't, it is engender'd; Hell and night
> Must bring this monstrous birth to the world's light.'[35]

He spends his time listening, observing, feeling his way in almost constant proximity to Othello until his plan materialises. In Act III he finally judges the scene set to bring out his strongest weapon:

Iago.   She did deceive her father, marrying you;
                And when she seem'd to shake and fear your looks,
                She lov'd them most.
Othello.   And so she did.
Iago.   Why, go to then,
                She that so young could give out such a seeming,
                To seal her father's eyes up, close as oak,
                He thought 'twas witchcraft: . . . .[36]

We see here a significant change in Iago's understanding of Othello. At the beginning of the play he offers us a description of Othello which is little more than a caricature and Iago's attempts against him are at this stage on par with this shallow understanding. Gradually, as his understanding develops, so does his imaginative approach to ways of achieving his purpose. His hatred does not prevent him from seeing Othello as he really is. On the contrary, it sharpens his perception to the extent where, in spite of his hatred, he is able to realise that Othello is of a constant, noble, loving nature and that his marriage is of the happiest:

> 'I dare think he'll prove to Desdemona
> A most dear husband.'[37]

The tragedy is that Othello does not really understand Iago, he knows and understands him only in his role of an honest, courageous soldier, not as a person. He does, however, apply this understanding to Iago's every action. Iago, by now, realises all too well this gullibility on Othello's part, his 'free and open nature', and makes full use of it. The important point is that Iago's hatred makes his understanding as acute as is possible to a man of his natural limitations; it enables him to realise to the full his potentiality for understanding. But the complexities of the personal understanding which Shakespeare tries to convey are such that they naturally give rise to constant controversies of interpretation. We can only go by what the text has to reveal to us. What is, perhaps, interesting is that Iago's limitations are due, in large measure, to his inability or non-comprehension of love. For him love is 'a mere lust of the blood and permission of the will'. Thus he perceives jealousy in relation to his definition and is, therefore, genuinely frightened at Othello's display of passion, his depth of feeling, his uncontrollable fury. But yet, when Othello says:

'Yet she must die, else she'll betray more men.'[38]

he shows us that Iago has succeeded, he has compelled Othello to rationalise in the way he does himself. Iago's success reveals to us how wholly he has 'placed' Othello. What better proof of this than that he succeeded in compelling Othello to act strictly within Iago's own field of understanding—suddenly Othello is behaving exactly as Iago thinks man should behave.

6.4 Conclusion

I hope that I have succeeded, with the help of the examples chosen, to bring out three main points:

1. That we cannot really understand ourselves and others without understanding the part emotions play in a person's view of the world and the role they play as springs of our actions. Understanding another's emotions and feelings and how these affect him is an important part of understanding him. This kind of understanding also involves understanding the way in which emotions enter, provoke and influence the development of understanding of persons within personal relationships.

2. That the *quality* of the understanding with which we have here been concerned cannot be captured exclusively in the form

G*

of knowledge/understanding that . . .; often, it cannot be adequately verbalised. Trying to verbalise the understanding is tantamount to interpreting and simplifying something which, through such an attempt, is lifted out of its crucial context— the personal relationship from which the understanding stems; it is to change *the quality* of the understanding.

3. That we are now also in a position to offer an answer to the question posed at the beginning of this chapter: Given that a certain kind of deep understanding of another is only possible within a personal relationship, what is it that a person, stand- ing in such a relationship with another, is able to understand that another person, who does not stand within a personal relationship with that other, is precluded from understanding?

The person who stands in a personal relationship with another is able to achieve deep understanding through being made aware of new possibilities within the context such relationships provide. What it is that is understood falls within the complex descriptions of the experienced situations as illustrated by the examples given. A person who stands outside a personal relationship is deprived of the context provided by such relationships. He can, therefore, be merely informed by one of the persons concerned. But, as I have argued, in trying to express something of the deep under- standing two people have of each other there is always the risk that one will not succeed in conveying that understanding to a third person. This is mainly because such understanding is very closely tied to the history of both persons, their background experiences, the growth and development of the situation in which they find themselves and such considerations as I have discussed when explicating the notion of 'situation' as an object of under- standing. There is also a crucial difference between having such understanding and trying to convey it. Two people's deep under- standing of each other manifests itself within their relationship which is its natural home. Trying to express something of this understanding is trying to shift it from its natural habitat with the accompanying difficulties.

The kind of understanding which persons can achieve within personal relationships is made possible by what can be summed up as the expressiveness or significance which persons possess for each other. This includes the variety of attitudes, feelings, inter- actions and responses which take place within a personal relationship. Much of the interaction and the responses are spontaneous and this feature of spontaneity with its quality which is akin to impact, is essential, as I have tried to show. Lack of impact and, often, lack of any feeling elicits lack of response and thus the power which provokes understanding is lacking.

A very good example of how such a lack completely inhibits any possibility of understanding is given by Virginia Woolf. She describes two people at a party who have reached the stage of running out of small talk:

> So things came to an end. And over them both came instantly that paralysing blankness of feeling, when nothing bursts from the mind, when its walls appear like slate; when vacancy almost hurts, and the eyes petrified and fixed see the same spot—a pattern, a coal scuttle—with an exactness which is terrifying, since no emotion, no idea, no impression of any kind comes to change it, to modify it, to embellish it, since the fountains of feeling seem sealed and as the mind turns rigid, so does the body; stark, statuesque, so that neither Mr. Serle nor Miss Anning could move or speak, and they felt as if an enchanter had freed them, and spring flushed every vein with streams of life, when Mira Cartwright, tapping Mr. Serle archly on the shoulder, said:
> 'I saw you at the *Meistersinger*, . . . that I should ever speak to you again.'
> And they could separate.[39]

This is a vivid example of what can happen when one is required to be on certain terms with another individual and finds that it is impossible. Lack of response and feeling can result in a paralysing blankness and thus blankness where understanding is concerned.

As I said above, the understanding which two people have of each other manifests itself within the personal relationship which exists between them. The difficulties encountered with third person understanding (persons standing outside the relationship) fall into two main kinds:

1. A person standing in the personal relationship can convey something he has of the understanding to a third person. But conveying such understanding requires an expression of that understanding in language. Expression in such cases is tied to language whereas expression within a relationship is tied also to action, interaction, feelings, response, etc. Expressing or

reporting such understanding to a third person turns such understanding into a reported as opposed to a lived experience. One has to rely on reports of others, reports which are outside the context of the personal relationship itself which provides the vital check of correctness or incorrectness of understanding.

2. The understanding two people have of each other within a personal relationship develops within a continuous, lived experience. The crucial point is that personal understanding is dependent on the significance two people have for each other and which exhibits itself spontaneously in personal relationships. This is not to say that a third person standing outside the relationship could not come to see or understand something of that significance but what he would understand would be an understanding out of context and, therefore, qualitatively different.

The quality of understanding within personal relationships is different from any understanding which a person standing outside such a relationship could ever achieve. It is an understanding which develops continually, which is very dependent on previous understanding and so on. Thus the crucial difference between the understanding which persons have for each other within a personal relationship and that which a third person can achieve is not so much a difference between *what* it is they understand; the crucial difference is in the quality of the understanding.

Personal relationships which supply the vital context in which deep understanding can take place also serve to underline the main difference between what is involved in our understanding of objects as opposed to our understanding of persons—persons are unique in forming personal relationships and any understanding of persons is dependent on our understanding of what this crucial fact involves.

Notes

1 J. Conrad, *Chance*, Dent's Collected Edition, 1949, p. 247.
2 J. Bayley, *The Characters of Love*, London, 1960, p. 5.
3 H. James, 'The Lesson of Balzac', in *The House of Fiction*, ed. L. Edel, Rupert Hart-Davis, London, 1957, p. 77.
4 J. Conrad, *Within the Tides*, Dent & Son, 1950, Author's note, p. viii.
5 J. Bayley, *op. cit.* p. 205

6 J. Benson, 'Emotion and Expression', *Philosophical Review*, (1967), pp. 335-57.
7 A. Solzhenitsyn, 'One Word of Truth', in *The Nobel Speech on Literature*, The Bodley Head, 1970, p. 14.
8 J. Conrad, *Chance, op. cit.* p. 88.
9 J. P. Sartre, *L'imaginaire*, Librairie Gallimard, Paris, 1940.
10 L. Tolstoy, *What is Art?*, trans. Aylmer Maude, Oxford University Press, 1959.
11 George Eliot, *Middlemarch*, Oxford University Press (497), 1959.
12 *Ibid.* p. 5.
13 *Ibid.* p. 89.
14 *Ibid.* p. 62.
15 *Ibid.* p. 225.
16 *Ibid.* p. 448.
17 *Ibid.* p. 515.
18 *Ibid.* p. 225.
19 *Ibid.* p. 390.
20 H. James, *The Wings of the Dove*, The Century Library, Eyre & Spottiswoode, 1948.
21 *Ibid.* pp. 76-7.
22 *Ibid.* p. 82.
23 *Ibid.* pp. 205-6.
24 *Ibid.* p. 206
25 *Ibid.* p. 325.
26 *Ibid.* p. 348.
27 *Ibid.* p. 370.
28 *Ibid.* pp. 413-14.
29 E. M. Forster, *A Room with A View*, Edward Arnold, 1962.
30 *Ibid.* pp. 57-9.
31 *Ibid.* p. 66.
32 *Ibid.* pp. 246-50.
33 W. Shakespeare, *Othello*, Act I, Scene 1, L. 58-65.
34 *Ibid.* Act I, Scene 3, L. 292-3.
35 *Ibid.* Act I, Scene 3, L. 397-402.
36 *Ibid.* Act III, Scene 3, L. 210-14.
37 *Ibid.* Act II, Scene 1, L. 285-6.
38 *Ibid.* Act V, Scene 2, L. 6.
39 Virginia Woolf, *Mrs Dalloway's Party* (A short story sequence by Virginia Woolf), ed. Stella McNichol, Hogarth Press, London, 1973, Chapter 5, 'Together and Apart', pp. 54-5.

7 Concluding Remarks

THE main question, to the answer of which I hope I have at least provided something of an introductory approach, is the philosophical question: 'How is it possible that human beings come to understand each other in various degrees in spite of the problems inherent in what human beings are?'

I have tried to search for possible answers by examining what is involved in our attempts to understand other persons and ourselves. In the course of the analysis the significance of the notion of objectivity for making knowledge possible was apparent. I also attempted to bring out the importance of subjective elements in our understanding and to show how these enter into our contact with others within the crucial framework of objectivity. This approach, I suggest, can be taken as an example of combining Bruner's gifts carried by the right and by the left hand, in the area of person understanding.

My main concern was to give an account of person understanding not tied to the usual private/public or internal/external distinctions. I have, therefore, approached this topic through an analysis of the concept of understanding in general followed by a detailed examination of particular cases of understanding within personal relationships.

The book incorporates four main strands of argument leading to the following conclusions:

1. That in any case of understanding two kinds of understanding are involved—the objective and the personal.
2. That situations are paradigmatic subject matter of understanding and that, conversely, an account of understanding can be given in terms of situation understanding.
3. That standing in a personal relationship with another person is a necessary condition of understanding him on a deep level.
4. That emotions and emotion concepts play a central role in both self and other understanding and cannot be treated as purely or necessarily passive phenomena which are also, therefore, irrational. A human being could not be intelligible to us

as an agent quite independently of this important emotional dimension.

These conclusions and the arguments leading up to them form the substance of my treatment of the topic of person understanding.

Implicit in the book is the view that one only has the possibility of being subjective within the limits of objectivity; the objective framework is basic to subjective/personal variations. The important point, which I hope I have succeeded in bringing out, is that the difficulties arising from our attempts to understand persons are not tied to what one can and what one can never come to understand but *how* one comes by such understanding. A real understanding of another person, as the person that he is, is only possible within personal relationships. The crucial difference between the understanding which persons have for each other within a personal relationship and that which a third person can achieve is not so much a difference between *what* it is they understand; the crucial difference is in *the quality* of the understanding. The difference stems from the way in which understanding is achieved.

In providing an elucidation of how it is possible that persons come to understand each other and the self in various degrees, I have attempted a philosophical account of understanding of the self and of other persons. I have tried to draw attention to the possibility of treating a certain phenomenon in a certain way—in a way which shows something of the nature of the phenomenon in question and what I take to be its very characteristic aspects.

In concentrating on the crucial notion of personal relationships I have tried to bring out the vitality such relationships provide for the possibility of understanding persons and thus understanding the self.

Bibliography

Allport, G. W. 'The Use of Personal Documents in Psychological Science', *S.S.R.C. Bulletin*, No. 49 (1942), p. 159.

Aristotle. *De Anima*, trans. D. W. Hamlyn, Clarendon Aristotle Series, ed. J. L. Ackrill, 1968.

——. *Nicomachean Ethics*, in *The Basic Works of Aristotle*, trans. R. Mckeon, Random House.

Bayley, J. *The Characters of Love*, London, 1960.

Benn, S. I. 'Freedom, Autonomy and the Concept of Person', *PAS*, Vol. LXXVI (1975/76), pp. 109-30.

Benson, J. 'Emotion and Expression', *Philosophical Review* (1967), pp. 335-57.

Berne, E. *Games People Play*, Penguin Books, 1971.

Bouwsma, O. K. 'The Expression Theory of Art', in *Aesthetics and Language*, ed. W. Elton, Basil Blackwell, Oxford, 1954, pp. 73-99.

Bruner, J. *On Knowing: Essays for the Left Hand*, Harvard University Press, 1962.

Collingwood, R. G. *The Idea of History*, Oxford, 1946.

——. *The Principles of Art*, Oxford University Press, 1960.

Conrad, J. *Chance*, Dent's Collected Edition, 1949.

——. *Within the Tides*, Dent & Son, 1950.

Eliot, G. *Middlemarch*, Oxford University Press, 1959.

Elliott, R. K. 'The Critic and the Lover of Art', in *Linguistic Analysis and Phenomenology*, ed. S. C. Brown and W. Mays, Macmillan, 1971, pp. 117-27.

Eliot, T. S. *Four Quartets*, Faber and Faber, London, 1972.

——. 'The Waste Land', *The Complete Poems and Plays of T. S. Eliot*, Faber and Faber, London, 1978.

Forster, E. M. *A Room with a View*, Edward Arnold, 1962.

Geach, P. *Mental Acts*, Routledge and Kegan Paul, 1957.

Goethe, J. W. von 'A Contribution to Optics', in *Pure Colour*, by Maria Schindler, New Culture Publications, London, 1946.

——. 'Dieselbe', in *Goethe's Poems*, ed. C. W. Eastman, Appleton-Century-Crofts Inc., New York, 1941, p. 47.

Gombrich, E. *Art and Illusion*, New York, 1960.

Goodman, N. *Languages of Art*, Harvester Press, 1977.

Hamlyn, D. W. 'Person-perception and Our Understanding of Others', in *Understanding Other Persons*, ed. T. Mischel, Basil Blackwell, Oxford, 1974, pp. 1-36.

——. *The Theory of Knowledge*, Anchor Books, Doubleday & Co., New York and Macmillan, London, 1970.

Hampshire, S. 'Subjunctive Conditionals', *Analysis* (1948), pp. 9-14.

Hegel, G. W. F. *Phenomenology of Mind*, trans. J. B. Baillie, revised 2nd edition. The Muirhead Library of Philosophy, George Allen & Unwin Ltd., 1949.

——. *Philosophy of Mind*, trans. W. Wallace, Clarendon Press, 1971.

Hesse, H. *Narziss and Goldmund*, trans. G. Dunlop, Penguin, 1973.

Hudson, L. *Human Beings*, Paladin, 1978.

——. *The Cult of the Fact*, Jonathan Cape, 1972.

Hugo, V. *Les Misérables*.

James, H. 'The Lesson of Balzac', in *The House of Fiction*, ed. L. Edel, Rupert Hart-Davis Ltd., London, 1957, pp. 60-85.

——. *The Wings of the Dove*, The Century Library, Eyre & Spottiswoode, 1948.

Jaspers, K. *Reason and Existenz*, trans. W. Earle, New York, 1955.

Kant, I. *Critique of Pure Reason*, tr. N. Kemp Smith, Macmillan, 1934.

——. *Critique of Judgement*, tr. J. H. Bernard, Hafner, London and New York, 1968.

Malcolm, N. *Ludwig Wittgenstein—A Memoir*, Oxford University Press, 1958.

Meehl, P. E. *Clinical versus Statistical Prediction*, University of Minnesota Press, Minneapolis, 1958.

Merleau-Ponty, M. 'L'Oeil et l'esprit', in *Art de France*, Vol. 1 No. 1 (Jan. 1961).

——. 'Eye and Mind', trans. Carleton Dallery, in *The Primacy of Perception and Other Essays*, ed. J. Edie, Northwestern University Press, 1964, pp. 159-90.

——. *Phenomenology of Perception*, trans. C. Smith, Routledge and Kegan Paul, 1962.

——. *Le Visible et l'invisible*, ed. Gallimard, Paris, 1964.

——. *The Visible and the Invisible*, trans. A. Lingis, ed. C. Lefort, Northwestern University Press, 1968.

Munroe, R. 'An Experiment in Large Scale Testing by a Modification of the Rorschach Method', *Journal of Psychology* (1942), pp. 229-63.

Penelhum, T. 'Pleasure and Falsity'—Symposium, *American Philosophical Quarterly*, Vol. 1 No. 2 (April 1964), pp. 81-91.

Peters, R. S. 'Emotions and the Category of Passivity', *PAS*, Vol. LXII (1961/62), pp. 117-34.

——. 'Personal Understanding and Personal Relationships', in *Understanding Other Persons*, ed. T. Mischel, Basil Blackwell, 1974, pp. 37-65.

——. 'Reason and Passion', in *The Proper Study*, Royal Institute of Philosophy Lectures, Vol. IV, 1969/70, Macmillan, 1971, pp. 132-53.

Popper, K. R. *Objective Knowledge*, Oxford, 1972.

Proust, M. *Du Côté de Chez Swann*, Vol. 2, ed. Gallimard, Paris, 1945.

——. *Swann's Way*, trans. C. K. Scott-Moncrieff, Penguin, 1971.

Sartre, J. P. *L'imaginaire*, Librairie Gallimard, Paris, 1940.

Schleifer, M. 'Psychological Explanations and Interpersonal Relations', in *Philosophy and Personal Relations*, ed. A. Montefiore, Routledge & Kegan Paul, 1973, pp. 170-90.

Shakespeare, W. *Othello*.

——. *King Lear*.

Solzhenitsyn, A. 'One Word of Truth', in *The Nobel Speech on Literature*, The Bodley Head, 1970.

Storr, A. 'The Master Mind', *Observer Magazine*, 12 July 1970, pp. 5-17.

Strawson, P. F. 'Freedom and Resentment', in *Studies in the Philosophy of Thought and Action*, ed. P. F. Strawson, Oxford, 1968, pp. 71-96.

Thalberg, I. 'Mental Activity and Passivity', *Mind*, Vol. LXXXVII, No. 347 (July 1978), pp. 376-95.

Tolstoy, L. *War and Peace*.

——. *What is Art?*, trans. Aylmer Maude, Oxford University Press, 1959.

Wittgenstein, L. *Philosophical Investigations*, trans. G. E. M. Anscombe, Basil Blackwell, Oxford, 1963.

Wollheim, R. 'Expression', in *Royal Institute of Philosophy Lectures*, Vol. 1, Macmillan, 1968, pp. 227-44.

Woolf, V. *Mrs. Dalloway's Party* (A short story sequence), ed. S. McNichol, Hogarth Press, London, 1973.

Index

(For specific books, poems, etc. *see* Literary examples.)